SEASON OF MIGRATION TO THE NORTH

Tayeb Salih

AUTHORED by Abigail Lind
UPDATED AND REVISED by Bella Wang

COVER DESIGN by Table XI Partners LLC
COVER PHOTO by Olivia Verma and © 2005 GradeSaver, LLC

BOOK DESIGN by Table XI Partners LLC

Published by GradeSaver LLC, www.gradesaver.com

First published in the United States of America by GradeSaver LLC. 2011

ISBN 978-1-60259-257-5

Printed in the United States of America

For other products and additional information please visit http://www.gradesaver.com

Table of Contents

Table of Contents

Biography of Salih, Tayeb (1929-2009)

Tayeb Salih was born in 1929 in rural Karmakol, in northern Sudan. He studied at the University of Khartoum, but there is no record that he graduated (Lalami). Like the narrator of *Season of Migration to the North*, Salih worked as a teacher in Sudan, before working for the BBC Arabic Service. He then worked in a variety of diplomatic positions, including as the director general of the Ministry of Information in Doha, Qatar, and as representative to the Gulf States for the United Nations Educational, Scientific, and Cultural Organization (UNESCO).

After years of success as a diplomat and education advocate, Salih published *Season of Migration to the North* in 1969. The novel won immediate accolades from critics worldwide, and it remains his most famous book, alongside the novella *The Wedding of Zein*. Despite this critical acclaim, most of Salih's work remains untranslated. His collected works, which include political essays, travel writing, and book reviews, are popular and widely available in Arabic. Even so, Salih remained a controversial figure into his old age, publishing an essay in 1990 that was sharply critical of the Islamist regime in charge of Sudan at the time. He died in 2009.

About Season of Migration to the North

Tayeb Salih published *Season of Migration to the North* in 1966, ten years after Sudan received its independence from the British empire on January 1, 1956. The novel is heavily influenced by the tumultuous politics of the period. The 1950s and 1960s saw many African countries achieve independence, some through bloody revolutions, and others through peaceful diplomacy. Initially there was much hope that Sudan would use the infrastructure developed by their European occupiers to turn their nations into prosperous, democratic havens for their long-oppressed citizens.

It was not long before these hopes were dashed. Negotiations for Sudanese independence had not addressed whether a federal or a unitary government would run the country. The ethnically separate southern part of Sudan favored a federal government, but the military regime in charge of the country immediately broke its promise to provide this, favoring instead a dictatorship run by northerners. Civil war broke out in 1955, even before the country had been officially granted independence. This bloody war would continue until 1972, and while the conflict is not explicitly addressed in Salih's novel, its shadow hangs over the villagers' stubborn hope for an efficient and democratic government.

Salih wrote *Season of Migration to the North* with an international audience in mind, and worked closely with his English translator, Denys Johnson-Davies, on translating bits and pieces of the novel before he even finished. Salih was equally fluent in English and Arabic, but felt obliged to write in Arabic as an expression of his national identity. The novel received critical acclaim across the globe upon its release, and has been translated into 30 languages.

The novel, along with Salih's other work (much of which remains untranslated) was popular as well among Arab audiences. However, it was banned in Sudan starting in 1989, although this was not because of the novel's politics but rather due to its graphic sexual content, which offended the Islamic government. However, it is now widely available in Salih's home country, and he is revered as a founding father of Sudanese literature.

Character List

The narrator's grandfather (Hajj Ahmed)

The narrator's nonagenarian paternal grandfather lives a happy, stable life of prayer and socializing. To both the narrator and Mustafa Sa'eed, the grandfather represents the simple, virtuous country life that they yearn for. Although the narrator never calls his grandfather by name, we eventually learn that it is Hajj Ahmed.

The narrator

The unnamed narrator of *Season of Migration to the North* was born in a normal farming family in Wad Hamid. However, his sharp intelligence and ambition allowed him to advance through the Sudanese education system and eventually attend university in London, where he earned a doctorate in British poetry. The narrator feels obliged to use his education to help advance Sudan, which had only been independent for 13 years when the novel was published. However, he finds this difficult because of his passive personality and widespread government corruption.

The narrator's father

A relatively minor figure in the novel, the narrator's father is kind and supportive to him. However, he is fundamentally conservative and cannot understand the narrator's objections to the oppression of women in village culture.

Mustafa Sa'eed

Mustafa Sa'eed looms in the narrator's thoughts throughout the novel. In his forties, Mustafa moved to Wad Hamid and remained a mysterious figure there, marrying a village woman, Hosna bint Mahmoud, but never speaking to anyone about his past. The narrator eventually learns that Mustafa is quite similar to himself—both men were highly intelligent as children, and attended university in the United Kingdom. However, while the narrator returned to Sudan and pursued a benign (if ineffectual) life of civil servitude, Mustafa Sa'eed tried to be an academic in the United Kingdom. His career was ruined after a series of sordid love affairs that culminated in Mustafa murdering his English wife, Jean Morris.

Mahmoud

A prominent farmer in Wad Hamid, Mahmoud arranges the marriage between his daughter, Hosna, and Mustafa Sa'eed. Many of the village elders, including the narrator's grandfather, judge Mahmoud for marrying his daughter to an outsider, but Hosna and Mustafa have a happy life together until the latter dies.

The eldest son of Hosna and Mustafa is also named Mahmoud, but he plays a very small role in the novel.

Wad Rayyes

A lifelong womanizer, Wad Rayyes is in his late forties when the narrator first returns from Europe, and is in his seventies in the 'present-day' section of the novel. Although he already has several wives, he is determined to marry Hosna Bint Mahmoud after her husband dies.

Mahjoub

The narrator's good friend from elementary school. Mahjoub was cleverer than the narrator as a child, but didn't pursue secondary school because he wanted to be a farmer. As an adult, he is the chairman of the Agricultural Project Committee and a major figure in village politics.

Bint Majzoub

Bint Majzoub is famous in the village for her willingness to speak bluntly about sex. Now in her eighties, Bint Majzoub successively married five husbands when she was younger, each of whom died. She is the only village woman who drinks and socializes with the men, and her best friends are Wad Rayyes, Bakri, and the narrator's grandfather. Bint Majzoub is the first person to hear Hosna's screams on the night she murders Wad Rayyes, and she assumes that Hosna is screaming from an orgasm.

Hosna bint Mahmoud

The beautiful, modest wife of Mustafa Sa'eed. After Mustafa dies, she lives alone and cares for her two sons, rejecting all suitors. As the executor of Mustafa's estate, the narrator is technically her guardian, although he feels uncomfortable with this role. When Wad Rayyes proposes to Hosna, the narrator realizes he is in love with her but does not intervene to stop the marriage. Hosna resists being forced to marry Wad Rayyes, and eventually murders him.

Sa'eed

Hosna and Mustafa's youngest son, named for his father. Not to be confused with Sa'eed the shopkeeper.

Sa'eed the shopkeeper

A village man.

Mr. Stockwell

The headmaster of Mustafa Sa'eed's elementary school in Khartoum.

Mr. Robinson

The headmaster of Mustafa Sa'eed's secondary school in Cairo. He is fascinated by the Arabic language and architecture. He takes Mustafa under his wing, giving him room and board and showing him around Cairo.

Mrs. Robinson

The kindly wife of Mr. Robinson, who takes Mustafa Sa'eed under his wing when the latter is in secondary school. Mustafa develops a crush on Mrs. Robinson, and remembers her fondly throughout adulthood.

Jean Morris

Mustafa's cruel, manipulative first wife. She continually rejects and humiliates him as a suitor, and then abruptly agrees to marry him. They have a fraught and tumultuous relationship, and eventually he stabs her to death while having sex with her.

Ann Hammond

A privileged twenty-year-old student of Oriental languages at Oxford, and Mustafa Sa'eed's first girlfriend in Britain. She kills herself by gas and leaves a note blaming her death on Mustafa.

Sir Arthur Higgins

The Principal Prosecutor in Mustafa Sa'eed's trial for murdering Jean Morris. Mustafa took a course in criminal law at Oxford that was taught by him. Arthur Higgins is known as a womanizing bohemian, and had a friendly relationship with Mustafa before the trial.

Professor Maxwell Foster-Keen

A prominent right-wing figure in London, and Mustafa Sa'eed's former professor at Oxford. Despite his dislike of Mustafa (and bitterness toward Africans more generally), he earnestly defends him in his trial for murdering Jean Morris because it is an important case.

The Mamur

A "Mamur" is a generic title for a high-level civil servant. The narrator encounters a retired Mamur on a train, and in conversation discovers that he was a classmate of Mustafa Sa'eed. The Mamur shares his memories of Mustafa with the narrator, as well as his reflections on working as a tax collector during the British occupation of Sudan.

Richard

An Englishman who attended Oxford a few years after Mustafa Sa'eed and works at the Ministry of Finance in Khartoum.

Mansour

A left-wing Sudanese civil servant who argues with Richard at the party in Chapter 3.

Abdul Karim

One of the narrator's uncles. Although most men in the village only take one wife, Abdul Karim has been married several times, and has also had affairs.

Abdurrahman

One of the narrator's uncles.

Abdul Mannan

One of the narrator's uncles. He is cynical and believes that the government cannot do anything right.

Wad Baseer

The most accomplished engineer in Wad Hamid, who was put out of business when people started using store-bought doors in their houses and water pumps instead of water-wheels.

Wad Basheer

Not to be confused with Wad Baseer. Long dead, he was Bint Majzoub's favorite of her eight husbands.

Bakri

A friend of the narrator's grandfather. He takes a moderate stance on female circumcision, and tries to discourage Wad Rayyes from marrying Hosna, saying that Wad Rayyes ought to focus on preparing himself spiritually for death.

Mabrouka

Wad Rayyes's eldest wife. She is completely unfazed by his death, and believes he deserves his fate.

Sheila Greenwood

The daughter of Scottish coal workers, Sheila Greenwood is Mustafa's second girlfriend during his time in London. She is charming and innocent, and had an idyllic relationship with Mustafa until she kills herself upon realizing he does not intend to marry her.

Major Themes

The indifference of nature

Throughout *Season of Migration to the North*, the narrator meditates on the degree to which we are all at the mercy of nature. His grandfather, who has had a calm and successful life, could be killed in a flood just as easily as Mustafa Sa'eed was, and even the exciting party on the way to Khartoum feels minuscule in the vast desert. Ultimately, the strict moral code of Wad Hamid is not much different from the looser culture of Europe, because human agency is subject to nature. Although people try to tame nature through various methods (such as the water pumps), everything they try is futile. There is a parallel to this in the characters' attempts to grapple with their personal natures; Mustafa is ultimately unable to live a happy, simple village life, and the narrator is similarly unable to burn the private room or commit suicide, because he does not have violence or hatred in his nature.

Misogyny

The most obvious examples of misogyny appear in the shocking second half of the novel, which includes the graphic discussion of female circumcision, as well as Hosna's forced marriage to Wad Rayyes. Although Salih condemns the oppression of women in rural Sudan, his critique is not limited to his own country. The women that Mustafa meets in England are also subject to social restrictions; they are educated but cannot get jobs, and they are socially tainted by their sexual relationships with Mustafa (which partially explains their suicides). Even well intentioned characters like Mahjoub believe that women are incapable of making decisions for themselves. The narrator is the only character that challenges this orthodoxy, but he is ultimately unwilling to intervene in Hosna's marriage or speak out against female circumcision. The earnest, searing depictions of oppression and violence against women in African and European societies are the least ambiguous political "message" in the novel. Salih's portrayal of these issues amounts to a clear call to action against social orders that hurt and enslave women, no matter where they are in the world.

Communication between Eastern and Western cultures

Season of Migration to the North shows many characters who make earnest attempts to start a dialogue with people from other cultures. Mustafa's lectures on Arabic poetry and development economics are well attended, and Richard and Mansour have an involved debate about the best way for Sudan to become economically advanced. Nevertheless, these attempts at dialogue are often thwarted by miscommunication, sometimes intentional and sometimes not. Mustafa blatantly lies to English people who have a sincere (if misguided) interest in his culture, and does not bother trying to correct their misconceptions. In addition, the political debate that the narrator witnesses is futile because Richard refuses to acknowledge the validity of the "superstitious" Sudanese culture. Neither side takes the other's attempts to communicate seriously, which deepens the rift between the cultures and prevents them from reconciling on a national level.

Political participation versus passivity

The narrator has the most progressive political views in *Season of Migration to the North*. He believes that people should see the world and become acquainted with other cultures, and he is a strong proponent of women's rights. However, he rarely speaks his mind, and he does not intervene when he sees corruption, be it at the national level (at his job at the Ministry of Education) or the personal level (in the forced marriage of Hosna bint Mahmoud). Thus, his political enlightenment amounts to nothing, for all its virtues, because he is so passive. He has a foil in Mahjoub, who is an economic populist but conservative on social issues, who is heavily involved in village politics despite his lack of education. As the mayor of Wad Hamid, Mahjoub has the ability to save Hosna and prevent Wad Rayyes's murder, but chooses not to. Through him, Salih reveals another form of passivity that is rooted not in personal cowardice but in ignorance and hatred.

The drawbacks of modernization

The recurring image of the water pumps on the Nile is the most prominent symbol of industrial modernization, which gradually takes hold in Wad Hamid over the course of the novel. The water pumps bring wealth to their owners but do not affect the lives of the village people, and they rearrange the shape of the river, possibly causing the floods that kill Mustafa and many others. The character of Wad Baseer experiences modernization's downsides firsthand. The most experienced handyman in the village, he is put out of work when people begin buying store-bought door frames and farming machines. The narrator notes that Wad Baseer's craftsmanship is better and more durable, but that he cannot compete with the prices of mass-produced goods. Salih portrays modernization as a process that benefits the upper and middle classes, but only harms the poor farmers that live in villages. It polarizes the classes, with the rich getting richer from the new technology, and the poor losing their livelihood.

The unreliability of storytelling

When reading *Season of Migration to the North*, it is easy to forget that the story is not told by an objective narrator, but by a character with emotions and biases. He strategically omits parts of the story, which becomes clear in the final chapters, when we hear the especially graphic parts of Mustafa's life story that were left out of Chapter 2. This calls into question what other omissions the narrator might have made. Similarly, the narrator rarely quotes certain characters directly; the most dramatic example of this is Hosna bint Mahmoud, whose dialogue is almost entirely paraphrased by the narrator. This emphasizes her lack of agency, and suggests that even the progressive narrator has internalized certain misogynistic attitudes. Consider Hosna's lack of 'voice' in the text in contrast to Mustafa Sa'eed, whose words are quoted at length and repeated throughout the story. Salih highlights these discrepancies to show that the narrator of any story is always biased. The act of storytelling is itself an act of selection, with some events emphasized and some left out.

Institutional corruption

The narrator witnesses rampant corruption at his job, and several characters--most notably Mahjoub and the narrator's uncle, Abdul Mannan--believe that Sudan will never become a developed country because its leaders are too corrupt, and its elections too undemocratic. The unfinished hospital in Wad Hamid is symbolic of the failures of the national government, as well as the unrealized potential that Sudan has to heal the wounds left by imperialism. Good will is not enough to solve the problem; the narrator hates corruption but never acts to stop it. The only way to intervene, it seems, is to participate in politics on an individual and local level, as Mahjoub does.

Glossary of Terms

Agricultural Project Committee

A committee of villagers that regulates agriculture in Wad Hamid. Mahjoub is its president, and Mustafa Sa'eed serves on it.

arak

A type of liquor made from dates, popular among the village people.

Bedouin

A nomadic, desert-dwelling group of tribes. Arab in descent, they live all over North Africa, Sudan, and the Arabian peninsula.

bint

Arabic for "daughter of." Instead of surnames, the women of Wad Hamid use "bint" along with their father's first name. "Bint Majzoub," then, simply means "daughter of Majzoub;" we never learn her first name.

caravanserai

A special inn that has a large courtyard to host caravans.

circumcision ceremony

In many parts of Africa and the Middle East, boys are circumcised at the onset of puberty, and not in infancy like in the West. The ceremony is a rite of passage that shows the boy is becoming a man.

collects

Short prayers associated with a particular day or season, which are said before the main prayer. Used in both Islamic and Christian traditions.

diwan

Reception room in houses, used to entertain male guests.

Effendi

A title of courtesy, similar to "sir." Even older people use it to refer to the narrator, because he has a high-level government job.

ewer

A large water jug.

faience

Glazed ceramic pottery.

female circumcision

The practice of cutting or removing a woman's clitoris during childhood, for religious or cultural reasons. It remains prevalent in parts of Africa and Asia, and was even more common when Salih wrote *Season of Migration to the North* in 1966. The practice is illegal and extremely controversial in most Western countries, and many Western NGOs now focus on eradicating it abroad.

Hajj

The pilgrimage to Mecca, required of all Muslims who are healthy and can afford to go.

harraz

A tree whose wood is often used to construct houses in Sudan.

jibba

A long, collarless garment that people in Islamic countries wear over their clothes.

lorry

Term used in the U.K. and the Commonwealth for a truck.

Mamur

A high-level civil servant.

Omda

The chief of a tribe or village.

sunna

The part of Islamic law that regulates daily life.

wadi

A dry riverbed.

Short Summary

The unnamed narrator returns to his hometown, Wad Hamid, a small village near the Nile in northern Sudan, after studying in British poetry in London for seven years. He is glad to be back, but the village has changed since he left--most importantly, there is a new arrival, a mysterious middle-aged man named Mustafa Sa'eed. The narrator is unnerved by Mustafa and asks his family and friends about the man. Eventually, the narrator's grandfather reveals that Mustafa is from Khartoum, adding that he is a good farmer and neighbor but keeps to himself. He moved to Wad Hamid five years before, and married Hosna bint Mahmoud. Later, Mustafa visits the narrator at his home, introducing himself but remaining coy about his past.

The narrator is at a drinking session with his friend Mahjoub, who sees Mustafa walking by and pressures the older man to join them. Mustafa reluctantly does, and as he gets drunk, he begins to recite poetry in English. The narrator is shocked by this, and approaches Mustafa the next day asking where he learned to speak English. Mustafa initially insists that the poetry was drunken gibberish, but the next morning he returns to the narrator. Mustafa Sa'eed says that if the narrator swears he will tell no one, he will reveal his life story. The narrator eagerly agrees.

As a young boy growing up in Khartoum, Mustafa was a genius and quickly advanced through elementary school, which was all the education that was available in Sudan at the time. Although he was poor and fatherless, the headmaster of his school arranged for him to attend secondary school in Cairo, where his school's headmaster, Mr. Robinson, mentored him. Upon graduating, Mustafa was awarded a scholarship to Oxford, and quickly became the darling of the English literary and political scenes. He associated mainly with left-wing bohemians, although he secretly resented their silly misconceptions about "Oriental" culture. In fact, he exaggerated his African roots, making up stories about living in the jungle and charming snakes. This proved to be a very effective way of seducing women, and Mustafa became very promiscuous, promising to marry women and callously then callously breaking it off. Three of his girlfriends—Ann Hammond, Sheila Greenwood, and Isabella Seymour—committed suicide after Mustafa Sa'eed broke their hearts. However, Mustafa's twisted relationships with women culminated in his marriage to Jean Morris, a cruel and manipulative woman that he eventually murdered. He was imprisoned for seven years, and left England upon being released to live a simple farm life in Sudan.

The story returns to the narrator's perspective. He reveals that Mustafa Sa'eed disappeared during a flood. Although the villagers believe his death was an accident, the narrator privately speculates that Mustafa killed himself. Two years later, the narrator accepts a job at the newly formed Ministry of Education in Khartoum. He remains preoccupied with Mustafa's story for the next 25 years. He meets a variety of people in Khartoum, many of whom knew or heard of Mustafa Sa'eed. He also hears a variety of political opinions from his colleagues. He quietly disagrees with all of them, but does not speak out about his own opinions.

Although the narrator spends most of his time in Khartoum, he returns to Wad Hamid whenever he can get time off. After a long period away, he returns to the village, which is making fitful attempts at modernization. Some young people are demonstrating for the National Democratic Socialist Party, but most of the villagers are cynical and believe the government will never do anything to help people like them. We learn that the narrator has been made the executor of Mustafa Sa'eed's estate and the guardian of his wife, Hosna bint Mahmoud, and their two sons.

The narrator goes to visit his grandfather, who is drinking with his friends Bakri, Wad Rayyes, and Bint Majzoub. Bint Majzoub is a striking character; well into her eighties, she drinks and smokes like a man, and she likes to chat and make explicit jokes about sex. The men and Bint Majzoub banter about sex, and debate the virtues and drawbacks of female circumcision. Bint Majzoub supports the practice, because she believes it makes women work harder to please their husbands. Wad Rayyes comes down against it, citing theological arguments, but ultimately his opinion comes down to the fact that he prefers having sex with uncircumcised women. Bakri insists that the issue is blown out of proportion and does not matter either way, and the narrator and his grandfather are both quiet during the debate. After the guests leave, the narrator's grandfather reveals that Wad Rayyes is planning to ask the narrator for Hosna's hand in marriage.

The narrator is uncomfortable and angry that he has been asked to make choices for Hosna, whom he believes should decide for herself what to do. He goes to visit her, asking what she thinks of the proposal. Hosna adamantly rejects it, saying that she will never remarry, and if she is forced to, she will kill the husband and then herself. The narrator contemplates how beautiful she is. The next morning, Wad Rayyes inquires how the narrator's visit went. The narrator advises him to drop the proposal since Hosna is not interested. Insulted, Wad Rayyes angrily insists that he will marry Hosna anyway, since her father and brothers have already agreed to the union.

The narrator asks his friend Mahjoub for advice. Mahjoub laughs off the dilemma, saying that the narrator cannot change the social order of Wad Hamid, and Wad Rayyes will probably die soon anyway. Mahjoub also suggests that the narrator marry Hosna; this would resolve the situation and would make sense since he is already the guardian of her boys. The narrator is ambivalent about this, but as he leaves Mahjoub, he realizes that he is in love with Hosna.

The narrator does not intervene in the marriage, and decides to take a truck back to Khartoum instead of a boat. On the way, he becomes delirious from heat and thirst. He sees a group of soldiers who are on the way to arrest a tribal woman who murdered her husband. That night, the narrator and his driver rest with several other truck drivers. They dance and drink together, and he enjoys the impromptu party.

One month later, the narrator receives a telegram from Mahjoub with the news that Hosna is dead. He returns to Wad Hamid but the villagers are reluctant to tell him what happened. He eventually finds out the story from Bint Majzoub, whom he plies with whiskey. She reveals to him that Hosna's father beat her until she agreed to marry Wad Rayyes. The marriage was tense and Hosna refused to consummate it, much to her new husband's frustration. One night, Bint Majzoub heard screams coming from Wad Rayyes's house. She assumes that Hosna finally agreed to have sex with him and screamed in orgasm. As the shrieks go on, though, she becomes annoyed, then concerned, and enters the house when Wad Rayyes calls for help. She discovers the old man's body. Hosna has stabbed him to death. She lies dead on the floor also, with a knife in her heart and many bite marks all over her body.

Some of the women had tried to hold a funeral for Hosna, but Mahjoub, by now the mayor of Wad Hamid, banned it, saying that she did not deserve remembrance. The narrator confronts him about this and Mahjoub stands by his opinion, further insulting Hosna. The narrator attacks him, but is pulled away before he can strangle his friend.

The narrator wakes up after having fainted. He is consumed by grief and anger, and goes to Mustafa Sa'eed's house, opening the private room that has remained locked since Mustafa Sa'eed's death. The room is filled with English books and photographs of Mustafa's English mistresses. A portrait of Jean Morris hangs in a place of honor above the fireplace. The narrator recalls more of Mustafa's story, which was left out in his account at the beginning of the book. We learn more about his relationship with Jean Morris, who took pleasure in humiliating Mustafa and destroying his possessions. We find out that Mustafa murdered Jean Morris by stabbing her to death as they had sex, and she seemed to derive pleasure from being killed.

The narrator is disgusted that Mustafa never truly left his past behind, and considers burning the private room. However, he decides that doing so will not help anything, and instead goes to swim in the Nile. He contemplates allowing himself to drown, but is seized by a sudden desire for a cigarette. He decides that he would rather live, because he wants to spend more time with the few friends he has left, and take care of his duties in life. He swims toward the shore and begins to call for help.

Quotes and Analysis

"I preferred not to say the rest that had come to my mind: that just like us [the Europeans] are born and die, and in the journey from the cradle to the grave they dream dreams some of which come true and some of which are frustrated; that they fear the unknown, search for love and seek contentment in wife and child; that some are strong and some are weak; that some have been given more than they deserve by life, while others have been deprived by it, but that the differences are narrowing and most of the weak are no longer weak."

The narrator, Page 5

Here, Salih reveals one of the most important messages of the novel—that despite the differences wrought by culture and centuries of imperialism, individuals in Europe and the Islamic world are more alike than they are different. Although Europeans are blamed for the damage done by their occupation of Africa, the Sudanese politicians that come to power after the British leave are just as corrupt as their predecessors.

The fact that all of this remains unsaid is also significant. The narrator refrains from telling the villagers this more nuanced view of Europe, although he admits that at least Mahjoub is intelligent enough to understand it. The narrator's inability to speak out or act decisively is perhaps a result of the personality trait that leads him to wax rhapsodic like this—he is ultimately an aesthete, not an activist. Because he is a writer, his skill is to observe society, not to change it directly.

"These girls were killed not by Mustafa Sa'eed but by the germ of a deadly disease that assailed them a thousand years ago."

Professor Maxwell Foster-Keen, Page 29

Mustafa Sa'eed's defense attorney uses this argument to reduce his sentence for murdering Jean Morris and causing the suicide of three of his other lovers. The attorney, Professor Maxwell Foster-Keen, makes a systemic argument that the alienation between Western and Eastern cultures, caused by colonialism, is responsible for the deterioration of Mustafa's romantic relationships. Foster-Keen argues that Mustafa came to England expecting to be enlightened, only to find that London was just as barbaric as Sudan, and in this way Western civilization has disappointed him, and he should not be held culpable for his violence.

This argument attempts to place Mustafa's experiences and feelings into a broader historical narrative. Salih disapproves of this sort of reasoning, in which individuals are defined by their place in a broader sociocultural landscape. After all, Mustafa's girlfriends provoked his anger in the first place by reducing him to an Orientalist stereotype, and now his defense attorney is doing the same thing. Mustafa disagrees with this line of reasoning and explains, "I am no Othello. I am a lie" (29). See "Season of Migration to the North and Othello" for an in-depth explanation of the similarities between Mustafa and Othello, a classic Orientalist stereotype. Mustafa, though, rejects the stereotype and wishes only for death, so that "the lie" might be killed along with him.

"Over there is like here, neither better nor worse. But I am from here, just as the date palm standing in the courtyard of our house has grown in our house and not in anyone else's. The fact that they came to our land, I know not why, does that mean we should poison our present and future?"

The narrator, Page 41

Here, the narrator tries to explain his affinity for Sudan over Europe, even though he believes that the differences between the two places are ultimately insignificant. He decides that his great love for Wad Hamid derives from being born there. This is an implicit condemnation of people like Mustafa Sa'eed or the British colonists, who abandon their homelands and live like parasites in other parts of the world. In the early chapters of the novel, the narrator believes that the main difference between himself and Mustafa is that he loves his hometown and longs for it while traveling, while Mustafa has no ties to any home.

Despite this implicit criticism of the British, though, the narrator believes that it is better not to dwell on Sudan's colonial period and instead focus on the future.

"If Mustafa Sa'eed had chosen his end, then he had undertaken the most melodramatic act in the story of his life."

The narrator, Page 56

The concept of "melodrama" appears in several different contexts in *Season of Migration to the North*. In the preceding chapter, the narrator characterizes the British invasion of Sudan as "a melodramatic act." By using the same terms for Mustafa Sa'eed's possible suicide, Salih identifies Mustafa with a kind of reverse-imperialism. Just like the British, the character journeys to a faraway land, "conquers" its women, and commits acts of horrifying violence. Melodrama, then, is the opposite of the simplicity for which both Mustafa and the narrator strive.

By calling Mustafa's suicide "melodramatic," the narrator suggests that it is in character with his behavior in Europe, which makes sense on several levels. Most obviously, it shows continuity with the younger Mustafa's mental state, since Mustafa wanted to commit suicide as a young man but could not bring himself to do it. It also demonstrates a certain lack of consideration for others; by leaving Hosna alone with her children, Mustafa indirectly drives her to the same violent fate as Ann Hammond, Isabella Seymour, and Jean Morris—death at the hands of a lecherous man.

"The infidel women aren't so knowledgeable about this business as our village girls ... They're uncircumcized and treat the whole business like having a drink of water. The village girl gets herself rubbed all over with oil and perfumed and puts on a silky night-wrap, and when she lies down on the red mat after the evening prayer and opens her thighs, a man feels like he's Abu Zeid El-Hilali."

Bint Majzoub, Page 67

Bint Majzoub's opinions about female circumcision are highly problematic. She ties the village women's eagerness to please their lovers to their own inability to enjoy sex, despite the fact that Bint Majzoub is known for enjoying sex very much herself. This suggests two possibilities: 1) That Bint Majzoub is misrepresenting her views on female circumcision, perhaps so that she can better fit in with the men she drinks with; or 2) That Bint Majzoub's famous enjoyment of sex is faked. The strong implication that Bint Majzoub is herself circumcised seems to back up the second option, as it is very hard for circumcised women to have orgasms. This then invites the question of why a woman might fake enjoyment of sex in a society as conservative as Wad Hamid. It seems that Bint Majzoub does this because it allows her to participate in male society when she otherwise could not. Although she appears to be a liberated woman who enjoys sex for itself, this enjoyment may be a façade, in which case her relationship to sex is just as transactional as that of the more conventional women who use the promise of sex to secure a wealthy husband. The only difference is that Bint Majzoub is more concerned with social acceptance by men than with financial security, which she already has.

"'It's you who've succeeded, not I,' I would say to [Mahjoub] with genuine admiration, 'because you influence actual life in the country. We civil servants, though, are of no consequence. People like you are the legal heirs of authority; you are the sinews of life, you're the salt of the earth.'"

The narrator, Page 82

At the time this novel was written, Sudan had just achieved independence from Great Britain, and many citizens felt they should dedicate their careers to making the country wealthy, advanced, and self-sufficient. The narrator follows one path to do this—he studies in England, and it is assumed that he will come back use his knowledge to help improve Sudan. The narrator tries, but he is unable to affect the lives of average people because he does not work with them directly, and his travels have left him somewhat out-of-touch with the realities of village life.

Mahjoub, then, presents an alternative. He chose not to go to secondary school and became involved in farming and village politics. The narrator believes that Mahjoub has more influence than he does, and deserves to have power and authority. It is true that Mahjoub has had a more concrete impact on life in Wad Hamid than the narrator has. However, Mahjoub's advice about Hosna reveals a certain flaw in his "authority." He believes that the narrator should do nothing to prevent her marriage to Wad Rayyes, since Hosna's father already approved it. He accepts that men will always rule over women, and that 'peasants' like himself will never have a say in politics above the village level. Although the narrator lacks Mahmoud's direct involvement with politics, he is able to think more broadly about what society should be like, and ponders systemic social flaws that Mahmoud takes for granted. Salih, then, is suggesting that both types of leader are essential to improving the country, and there is a place for each.

"I became aware of [Hosna's] voice in the darkness like blade of a knife. 'If they force me to marry, I'll kill him and kill myself.'"

The narrator (quoting Hosna bint Mahmoud), Page 80

The obvious foreshadowing of the murder-suicide in this passage is paired with subtler hints of what is to come. The comparison of Hosna's voice to the blade of a knife is a clear allusion to the murder weapon, but it also evokes Mustafa's repeated comparison of his mind to "a sharp knife." Hosna, it seems, has embraced Mustafa's pairing of sex with violence, and indeed her murder of Wad Rayyes, which apparently happens while he is trying to rape her, echoes Mustafa's murder of Jean Morris, which occurs while they are having sex.

It is also interesting that the narrator compares Hosna's voice to the knife. Throughout the novel, the narrator has been unable to speak up when he sees something bad happening, be it corruption at the Ministry of Education or Hosna's forced marriage. In the novel, one's voice is equated with one's agency, so the comparison of Hosna's voice to a knife suggests that the only way for her to have a voice, to take control of her life, is through violence.

"How strange! How ironic! Just because a man has been created on the Equator some mad people regard him as a slave, others as a god. Where lies the mean? Where the middle way?"

The narrator, Page 89

Here, Salih addresses the contradictory attitudes that the British have toward the people they colonize. On the one hand, they mythologize them through Orientalist art and literature, but on the other, they treat them like animals and subjugate their countries. The one thing the British do not do is attempt to understand Easterners as fellow humans. Mustafa experiences this on an individual level in Britain; Isabella Seymour worships him and Jean Morris scorns him, but he does not have a healthy, equitable relationship with anyone. Within the novel, a "middle way" is illusory both in personal relationships and in politics; Westerners are always either romanticizing Eastern culture (like the Robinsons) or dehumanizing it (like Richard the finance analyst).

"I feel hatred and seek revenge; my adversary is within and I needs must confront him ... I begin from where Mustafa Sa'eed had left off. Yet he at least made a choice, while I have chosen nothing."

The narrator, Page 111

Here, the narrator finally acknowledges the parallels between himself and Mustafa Sa'eed. Both men have an "adversary ... within" as their ultimate nemesis, and confronting their own darker, violent natures is more of a challenge than dealing with their British or Sudanese enemies. Mustafa tried to fight his violent side by marrying Hosna and living a peaceful life in Wad Hamid, but ultimately he succumbed and committed suicide. By acknowledging that he faces the same demons, the narrator is able to learn from Mustafa's experiences, and reconcile himself with his own conflicted nature.

"[Isabella Seymour] had had eleven years of happy married life, regularly going to church every Sunday morning and participating in charitable organizations. Then she met him and discovered deep within herself dark areas that had previously been closed."

The narrator, Page 116

It is established in the rest of the novel that Mustafa Sa'eed and the narrator have violent alter egos that they constantly struggle to control. However, little has been said up to this point about the seemingly innocent victims of Mustafa's behavior. Isabella Seymour cheated on her loving husband to be with Mustafa, and Ann and Sheila abandoned their families. However, these acts of hedonism are mostly downplayed. In this instance, though, Salih acknowledges that Isabella too has "dark areas" that are exacerbated by Mustafa. By the end of the novel, it is clear that the battle between the peaceful and violent sides of one's self is not exclusive to Mustafa and the narrator, but is a dramatization of the conflicts that all people struggle with daily.

Summary and Analysis of Chapter 1

Summary

After seven years of studying in Europe, the unnamed narrator has returned to his hometown, Wad Hamid, a small village near the Nile in Sudan. Having become accustomed to the people and climate of Great Britain, the narrator at first feels uncomfortable after returning to the village. However, the sound of turtledoves cooing and the wind in the palm trees calms him, and he is reassured that "all was still well with life" (4). While having tea with his parents the morning after his return, the narrator recalls an unfamiliar, middle-aged man who stood silently in the crowd that welcomed the narrator back. His father explains that the man is Mustafa Sa'eed, a stranger who moved to Wad Hamid five years ago. Mustafa bought a farm and married Mahmoud's daughter, but he keeps to himself and no one knows much about him.

The narrator recalls seeing Mustafa among the crowd. The villagers had many questions about England—they want to know about the weather, how people make money, and if Europeans are immoral. The narrator replies that Europeans are the same as the villagers in every meaningful way. He wishes to expound further on this, but restrains himself because he believes the villagers are not intelligent enough to take his point. Throughout the gathering, Mustafa's silence and mysterious smile unnerve the narrator.

Forgetting about Mustafa, the narrator visits each family in the village to hear their news from the past seven years. He also visits his old childhood haunt, an acacia tree overlooking the Nile. The narrator reflects that as he grew up, he witnessed the shift from water wheels to water pumps, which changed the shape of the river, drying it up in some places and adding water in others. The narrator then goes to visit his grandfather, who is very knowledgeable about the people in Wad Hamid and its outlying areas. He asks him about Mustafa Sa'eed, but his grandfather only knows that the man is from Khartoum, and married Mahmoud's daughter, Hosna, a year after arriving in the village. The narrator's grandfather grumbles that Mahmoud's tribe "doesn't mind to whom they marry their daughters," but then qualifies this complaint by noting that Mustafa has always been a good citizen.

Two days later, Mustafa visits the narrator at his home, bringing fruit and explaining that he would like to get to know the narrator. The narrator notices that Mustafa's excessive politeness is uncharacteristic of village culture. In their conversation, the narrator reveals to Mustafa that he earned a doctorate in English poetry, but is offended when Mustafa replies that "we have no need of poetry here" and that he should have pursued a more practical subject that could help advance the country, like engineering or agriculture. The narrator changes the subject asking Mustafa about his origins in Khartoum. Mustafa becomes uncomfortable, but explains that he "did business" in Khartoum but wanted to try farming, and moved to Wad Hamid sight unseen based on instinct. He then leaves abruptly, saying to the narrator without further explanation: "Your grandfather knows the secret."

The narrator asks Mahjoub and his other friends about Mustafa, but learns nothing new. Two months later, Mahjoub invites the narrator to a meeting of the Agricultural Project Committee, which regulates farming in Wad Hamid. Mustafa is a member of the Committee, and demonstrates great charisma when he solves a disagreement about villagers allocating more water to their crops than they have been allotted.

Later, Mahjoub invites the narrator to a drinking session. When Mustafa walks by, Mahjoub pressures him to sit and drink with the men although it is clear Mustafa does not want to. Eventually Mustafa relents, and after getting drunk, he begins to recite from the poem "Antwerp" by Ford Madox Hueffer. The narrator is impressed and terrified by Mustafa's perfect English, and demands to know where he learned it. Mustafa storms out without saying a word. The next day, the narrator confronts Mustafa about the poetry, accusing him of hiding something about his identity. Mustafa shrugs off the incident, saying that the poetry was only drunken ranting and the narrator should not make too much of it.

The following day, Mustafa approaches the narrator, telling him that he has something to say and the narrator should come to Mustafa's house later. Curious, the narrator goes. Mustafa says that he will tell the narrator the truth about his identity so that he will not imagine things or tell the other villagers about his suspicions. After swearing the narrator to secrecy, Mustafa Sa'eed shows him his birth certificate and passport, which has stamps from many countries in Europe and Asia. He then begins to recount his life story.

Analysis

The opening chapter of Season of Migration to the North serves as a frame for the rest of the story. After this chapter, we will hear a monologue relating the story of Mustafa's life, before returning to the narrator's point of view many years later. Many of the insights that we learn about the narrator's character also shed light on Mustafa Sa'eed. For example, the narrator remains deeply conflicted about whether it is better to stay in Wad Hamid or to travel the world. Although he is curious about the world and about the knowledge it has to offer, he explains that "I hear a bird sing or a dog bark or the sound of an axe on wood—and I feel a sense of stability, I feel that I am important, that I am continuous and integral" (6). Unlike the narrator, Mustafa Sa'eed feels like an outcast during his childhood in Khartoum, and this lack of a positive cultural reference point might explain why he reacts so violently to British culture.

Also in this quote, Salih introduces a stereotype that many Westerners have about Islamic societies—that they are more communal and tightly knit than the great cities of Europe and America. Throughout the novel, Salih will continuously undermine this stereotype of village life, until neither the narrator nor the readers believe it any longer. By the end of Season of Migration to the North, it becomes clear that the villagers can be just as violent, cruel, and rigid as Western city-dwellers. Like Salih, Mustafa also enjoys playing on stereotypes, exaggerating his foreignness in order to pick up women. In a way, Salih is doing the same thing with his novel, creating an idyllic depiction of village life that he will then destroy by focusing on the gritty realities of poverty, colonialism, and the oppression of women.

The first chapter presents a broad view of political issues on which Salih will focus later in the story. The narrator remarks on the modernization of agriculture when he reflects on the replacement of water wheels with powerful, electric water pumps. "Seeing the bank contracting at one place and expanding at another," the narrator says, "I would think that such was life: with a hand it gives, with the other it takes" (6). This measured, pessimistic view of modernization is characteristic of Salih, whose characters often express doubts about whether modernization and freedom imperial rule will actually improve their lives.

In this section, Mustafa Sa'eed is established as a foil to the narrator; over the course of the novel, they will become more and more similar until eventually, it becomes unclear which of them is actually narrating the story. In the first chapter, though, Mustafa and the narrator seem very different—while Mustafa keeps to himself and resents being invited to drink with the village men, the narrator is a veritable social butterfly who spends most of the chapter calling on family and friends. Until the narrator sees the stamps in Mustafa's passport at the end of the chapter, he assumes that Mustafa is unintelligent and provincial, because he pretends not to know what a doctorate is.

This contrast between the two personalities heightens Mustafa's enigmatic allure, while also undercutting the narrator's authority as a storyteller. The narrator is unreliable in this section because he is fundamentally self-centered; he frequently admits to being egotistical and regarding himself as "the outstanding young man in the village." Because of his narcissism, the narrator tends to exaggerate the differences between him and the other characters, portraying Mustafa Sa'eed and others as parochial and unintelligent. In the case of Mustafa Sa'eed, the narrator is proved wrong at the end of the chapter, and the sudden revelation that Mustafa is in fact quite worldly invites readers to question whether the narrator's assessments of Mahjoub, Hosna, and his grandfather are equally inaccurate.

Summary and Analysis of Chapter 2

Summary

Mustafa Sa'eed begins to tell the narrator the story of his life. Mustafa is the only child of a camel trader from Khartoum, who died before he was born. He grew up alone with his mother, with whom he had a distant but cordial relationship, and was more independent and less emotional than other children were at his age. At this time (the early twentieth century), many Sudanese were afraid of the British efforts to establish schools for the natives, and would hide their children from government officials who came to enroll their children in school. However, Mustafa volunteers to go to school after seeing a government official; he likes the man's hat and wants to become a civil servant so he can wear one just like it. He remembers this as an important moment because "it was the first decision I had taken of my own free will" (20).

Aided by an excellent memory and a knack for problem solving, Mustafa quickly becomes the most brilliant student in his school, scorning the friendship of other boys to focus on intellectual pursuits. He repeatedly compares his mind to a sharp knife. When Mustafa is twelve, Mr. Stockwell arranges for him to go to high school in Cairo on a scholarship, as there are no high schools in Sudan. However, Mustafa feels no gratitude towards him. After an emotionless farewell to his mother, Mustafa Sa'eed heads for Cairo.

In Cairo, Mr. Robinson, the headmaster of Mustafa's new high school, meets the boy at the train station along with his wife, Mrs. Robinson. Mustafa recalls being aroused when Mrs. Robinson hugs him in greeting, and reflects that she would be his only friend after he was imprisoned for murder as an adult. For the next three years, the Robinsons, who speak Arabic and are interested in Islamic culture, take Mustafa to see important cultural sites around Cairo, and Mrs. Robinson introduces him to Western writers and composers.

At fifteen, Mustafa is accepted to university in London and sets sail for England. He reflects that his life in Cairo was largely dull, and he looks forward to exploring "unknown horizons" (25). Upon arriving in England, he notices that it lacks the hustle and bustle of Cairo—the geography is very orderly, and people are quiet and polite.

Mustafa's narrative now flashes forward, to when he first meets Jean Morris at a party ten years later. He is drunk but is stunned by her arrogance and cold beauty when she enters the room. By this time, Mustafa has immersed himself in the London literary and political scenes, and has made a hobby of seducing women. The second time he sees her, Jean Morris tells Mustafa that he has the ugliest face she has ever seen, and he resolves to "one day make her pay for that" (27). The next morning, Mustafa wakes up with his current girlfriend, Ann Hammond, a privileged twenty-year-old who studies Oriental languages at Oxford. Mustafa explains that he transformed the innocent girl "into a harlot" (27), and that one day she would gas herself to death, leaving a note that says, "Mr. Sa'eed, may God damn you" (27).

The story flashes forward again, to Mustafa Sa'eed's trial. He is charged with the murder of Jean Morris, as well as causing the suicides of Ann Hammond, Sheila Greenwood, and Isabella Seymour. Mustafa is defended by his former professor, Maxwell Foster-Keen, who argues that Mustafa and the women are all victims of a larger clash of civilizations, and Mustafa cannot be blamed for the murders because Western culture is less civilized than it should be. We also learn that Mustafa was made a lecturer in economics at London University at twenty-four, and became famous for his "appeal for humanity in economics" (31).

Mustafa doubles back to his early relationship with Jean Morris. After pursuing her relentlessly, Jean finally says that she cannot bear to be chased anymore, so they should get married. Their marriage is passionate and tumultuous, and to Mustafa, sex with Jean feels like an act of aggression.

His narration then goes on a tangent, as he remembers Sheila Greenwood. "A waitress in a Soho restaurant, a simple girl" (30), Mustafa is surprised that Sheila, a virgin when he met her, had the strength to commit suicide.

In another flashback, Mustafa recalls seeing a beautiful older woman, Isabella Seymour, at Speaker's Corner in Hyde Park. She reminds him of Mrs. Robinson. He invites her out for tea, which she accepts. To capture her interest, he makes up stories about "deserts of golden sands and jungles where non-existent animals call out to each other" (32-33). As they chat, she asks him about his race, to which he responds: "I am like Othello—Arab-African" (33). He lies to her about her name, saying that it is Amin Hassan.

Mustafa says to the narrator that the secret to happy life is simple living; this is the secret that the narrator's grandfather knows. However, Mustafa is condemned by his ambition to live a complicated, twisted life. Thinking back to Isabella Seymour, Mustafa reveals that she was resistant to his seduction at first, but after having sex with him, she told him that she loved him and promptly burst into tears.

Analysis

As Laila Lalami notes in her introduction to the New York Review Classics edition of the novel, Mustafa's relentless intellectualism helps explain his violence. Throughout the chapter, Salih sets up intellectual pursuit in opposition to the good things in life—compassion, simplicity, community. Not coincidentally, intellectual curiosity is what leads both Mustafa and the narrator to leave Sudan study in England. Mustafa's mind, like a "sharp knife," cuts past human emotion, and he finds he cannot appreciate the beauty of London when he arrives there (32). This is the source of an important difference between Mustafa and the narrator—while the narrator equates intellectualism with passion, imagination, and exciting experiences, Mustafa uses his academic studies to distance himself from all of these things.

This chapter also introduces Mustafa's method of seducing women. He fabricates details about life in Sudan, romanticizing his life story to reflect all the dreams, fears, and "hankerings" that British women have for the Eastern world. The women's credulous acceptance of Mustafa's lies illustrates a broader point tendency in Salih's portrait of race relations. Even well intentioned Westerners, like Ann Hammond and Isabella Seymour, cannot relate to Easterners as equals, because they prefer romantic fantasies about a wild "heart of darkness" to the truth, which is that Africans are not so different from Europeans.

Interestingly, Mustafa's anger toward the British women who are fascinated with his world does not extend to Mr. Robinson, who is also "interested in Islamic thought and architecture." (23) Unlike the women, Mr. Robinson does not study the Middle East from afar, but moves there with his wife and learns the language. Despite his anger, then, Mustafa's view of Westerners is not wholly damning; he only resents the ones who think they understand other cultures without really trying.

Stylistically, Mustafa's narration is much more sophisticated than that of the narrator. He repeats key phrases, comparing himself to a "sharp knife" and a "thirsty desert," and ending each anecdote with the refrain, "And the train carried me to Victoria Station and to the world of Jean Morris." This lends his narration an element of music or poetry, and associates it the African tradition of oral storytelling, while the narrator's story is much more linear and straightforward, having more in common with the self-consciously literary style of a British novel.

The portrayal of time in this section is also more fractured than the opening chapter. Mustafa flashes forward and backward in time; the chapter's rhythms mimic the free associations of human thought. One result of this structure is that it can be hard to tell the exact chronology of Mustafa's many affairs. This speaks to his casual attitude toward the individual women; they blur together in his narrative because they blur together in his mind. He only cares about sex, and the women are interchangeable, even when they kill themselves because he has broken their hearts. The vague chronology also develops a circular notion of time, in which important images and situations repeatedly occur, and no one ever truly escapes their past.

Summary and Analysis of Chapter 3

Summary

The story returns to the narrator's perspective. The narrator tells us that in July, an indeterminate amount of time after telling the narrator his life story, Mustafa disappeared while working in the fields during a flooding of the Nile. His wife was distraught and the villagers conducted an extensive search for him, but Mustafa's body was never found and everyone assumed that crocodiles ate him. The narrator is in Khartoum at the time and only hears of Mustafa's demise later.

The narrator returns to the night that Mustafa began his life story. After ending for the night, the narrator wanders around Wad Hamid. He passes Wad Rayyes' house and overhears him having sex with his wife; the narrator feels ashamed for invading the couple's privacy. He then reflects that although he knows the village intimately, he has never seen it so late at night. He passes his grandfather's house and hears the old man getting ready for morning prayers. After Mustafa's disturbing story, the narrator is comforted by his grandfather's immutable daily ritual.

The narrator reflects on the differences between himself and Mustafa. Although the narrator also slept with English women, he did so "superficially, neither loving nor hating them" (41). During his time in Britain, the narrator was often homesick and cherished his memories of Wad Hamid. He reiterates his belief that Europeans are fundamentally similar to Africans, and that after the British leave Sudan, the locals will simply pick up and continue their lives as if nothing had happened.

Two years after Mustafa's death, the narrator takes a job at the Department of Education in Khartoum. He remains preoccupied with Mustafa for the next 25 years. One day, on the train to an outlying city, the narrator encounters a retired Mamur who went to school with many important government officials. Reminiscing about his school days, the Mamur reveals that he also went to school with Mustafa, who was the most brilliant student in his year, but was known for being an aloof teacher's pet. He and his classmates were very jealous of Mustafa's talent for the English language. The Mamur then goes on a tangent, telling the narrator about his career as a tax collector before becoming a Mamur. He gripes that the Sudanese tax collectors would try to do their jobs, but people would often appeal their taxes to the English imperial government, which would grant the appeals, thus currying favor with the locals and sowing resentment for the Sudanese middle class, which consisted largely of low-level civil servants. He continues that the British government always gave the good bureaucratic jobs to "nobodies" (45), and because Mustafa was intelligent and his mother came from an obscure tribe, his classmates were sure he would go far.

Less than a month after meeting the Mamur, the narrator is at a party with other government officials. During a discussion about "mixed marriages" between Sudanese men and English women, a young lecturer from the university brings up

Mustafa Sa'eed. The lecturer gives a very different account of Mustafa's life, saying that he took British citizenship, was a major supporter of British imperialism and possibly a secret agent in the Middle East, served as a secretary at the British Naval Conference of 1936, and is now "a millionaire living like a lord in the English countryside" (46). The narrator calmly responds by giving a very specific inventory of the paltry estate that Mustafa left behind when he died. The lecturer is startled and asks if the narrator is Mustafa's son. The lecturer corrects himself since he knows that the narrator could not possibly be Mustafa's son, and laughs off the narrator's knowledge as a poet's "flight of fancy" (47), much to the narrator's annoyance. We also learn that the narrator was made into Mustafa's executor, and has taken charge of his two sons.

Richard then butts into the conversation, saying that Mustafa was a dubious economist who had a reputation for fudging his statistics and relying on generalities rather than facts. He adds that Mustafa was popular among left-wing bohemians, who embraced him as a kind of "token" African. The Englishman adds that if he had stuck to academics and avoided the leftists, Mustafa could have done great things for Sudan, a country that still clings to superstition. The narrator thinks to himself that Richard's statistics and Sudanese superstitions are merely different varieties of dogma, and that British colonialism was "a melodramatic act" (50) that is blown out of proportion by both sides.

Analysis

In this short chapter, Salih puts aside Mustafa's dark, mysterious narrative and returns to the narrator's inner world. While Mustafa is a violent, self-centered character, the narrator initially seems to be a "model Sudanese citizen" (Harss). However, this chapter foregrounds the narrator's passivity. When the young lecturer recounts a ridiculous, exaggerated version of Mustafa's life, the narrator makes a half-hearted attempt to refute it, but fails to explain Mustafa's true fate in a way that the party guests can understand, retreating into himself after listing the contents of Mustafa's will.

In this chapter, Salih presents a variety of opinions on the 77-year British occupation of Sudan. The Mamur represents the prejudices of the postcolonial Sudanese elite; although the free Sudan seems to be more progressive just because it is free of imperial war, Salih warns us against making this assumption. The Mamur is prejudiced against "nobodies" from obscure tribes or from Southern Sudan, and is annoyed that the British used a meritocratic model in awarding government positions, rather than giving them to the existing Sudanese aristocracy. After the British left, prejudiced individuals like the Mamur were once again allowed to rule, but the implicit question is whether this is actually better for the general population than foreign rule.

As with the Mamur, Mustafa Sa'eed provides Richard a point of departure to express his views about colonialism more broadly. An Englishman who has nevertheless remained in Khartoum after his country pulled out, Richard rejects the "superstitions" of the Sudanese and the bleary-eyed romanticism of his left-wing countrymen. He shares Mustafa's contempt for the Londoners who embrace him as a token of their own tolerance and liberalism. However, Salih identifies Richard's faith in statistics as merely another kind of religious dogma, and represents his condescension to Sudanese culture as an impassable "chasm" (50) that prevents him from having real dialogue with the African characters.

The Mamur and Richard attempt to engage in a meaningful dialogue about colonialism, but ultimately only express their own views. The narrator, however, does not even try to express his views, a passivity that undercuts the moral authority that he might otherwise have, given his sensitive and measured political opinions. The narrator's insistence on placing the Sudanese events within a very broad historical narrative seems in this chapter to be the correct point of view; he at least has an aesthetic appreciation of the experiences of ordinary Sudanese, and lacks the Mamur's prejudice or Richard's arrogance.

Nevertheless, the narrator's perspective will also be exposed as out-of-touch by the end of the book, and his inability to actively contribute to his country or intervene with an atrocity in his village will reveal the moral bankruptcy of the Sudanese elite's orthodox liberalism. Salih lays the groundwork for this exposure in the third chapter by establishing the narrator as fundamentally passive; although he initially seems to stand in opposition to the 'wrong' viewpoints of Richard and the Mamur, the differences between their ineffectual viewpoints will shrink in the context of the rest of the novel.

Summary and Analysis of Chapters 4 and 5

Summary

The narrator insists that despite his long discussion of Mustafa Sa'eed, he is not obsessed with the man. He compares life to a perpetually moving caravan, in which people cannot stop long to dwell on the dead. Although the narrator now works in Khartoum, he still spends two months per year in Wad Hamid, and the story turns to when the narrator is returning on just such a visit. The village has changed: The narrator passes an unfinished hospital that the government started to build and then abandoned, and a group of 'peasants' is rallying for the National Democratic Socialist Party. The narrator and his uncles express doubt that these developments will actually change the villagers' daily lives.

The narrator thinks back to Mustafa Sa'eed, who left the narrator an undated letter before he died. In the letter, he leaves his "wife, two sons, and all [his] worldly goods" (54) in the narrator's care. He stipulates that Hosna can do as she wishes with Mustafa's property, and that the narrator should simply make himself available to help the family and act as an adviser to his sons. Mustafa hopes that his sons will be spared "the pangs of wanderlust ... have a worthwhile upbringing and ... take up worthwhile work" (54). He also leaves the narrator the key to his "private room" where his diaries are kept, saying that although his life holds no useful lessons, the narrator is free to satisfy his curiosity now. The narrator had long suspected that Mustafa committed suicide, and the tone of the letter seems to confirm that.

In a part of Mustafa's story that is not revealed until now, we find out that Mustafa hoped to be executed at his murder trial, since he had wanted to commit suicide after killing Jean Morris but had not had the courage. He recalls that even Ann Hammond's father, one of the jurors, voted for life imprisonment instead of capital punishment, explaining that Ann might have killed herself for reasons unrelated to Mustafa. Mustafa also explicitly lied to Ann, telling her that they would marry so that she would have sex with him, and then went back on his promise. This was implied in Chapter 2.

The narrator contemplates the indifference of nature, which is ultimately what killed Mustafa, whether or not he intended it. He observes that the Nile flows inexorably to the north.

The narrator goes to visit his grandfather, who is drinking with Wad Rayyes, Bakri, and Bint Majzoub. As he enters his grandfather's home, he ponders that his grandfather is part of the natural world, and that the fate of the man and his beautiful house are both tied to vicissitudes of nature. Wad Rayyes is in the middle of a raunchy story about raping a slave girl when the narrator arrives. Bint Majzoub, an old woman who smokes and talks about sex with the men, teases Wad Rayyes and then talks about how much she enjoyed sex with one of her eight husbands, Wad Basheer. We learn that Bint Majzoub is very wealthy from the combined estates of her eight husbands, and that she is known for being "uninhibited in her conversation" (64).

Wad Rayyes, who is seventy but still handsome and libidinous, mentions that he hopes to take another wife. (Although Wad Hamid is a mostly monogamous village, rural Sudanese society at this time was polygynous, meaning that men could have multiple wives, but women could not have multiple husbands. Bint Majzoub married her eight husbands successively, after each one died.)

Wad Rayyes teases the narrator about having sex with infidel women, but the narrator is taciturn and says he does not know what Wad Rayyes is talking about. Bint Majzoub insists that circumcised village women are better lovers than their foreign counterparts are, because they view sex as something that only pleases the man, and thus put more effort into it. Wad Rayyes disagrees vehemently, saying that uncircumcised women are more fun when having sex. He argues that Muslims in other parts of the world do not circumcise their women, and they are just as faithful as the people of Wad Hamid, who do. Bakri says that women are the same everywhere, circumcised or not.

The men and Bint Majzoub continue to joke lewdly, and after having a hearty laugh, they all pray for God's forgiveness. Wad Rayyes invites the narrator to lunch. After he leaves, the narrator's grandfather reveals that Wad Rayyes did this because he plans to ask the narrator for Hosna Bint Mahmoud's hand in marriage. Because the narrator is the guardian of Mustafa's wife and children, he must approve Hosna's remarriage. The narrator complains about this, saying that he is only the guardian of Mustafa's children, and Hosna can do as she pleases. The grandfather retorts by saying that the narrator could still help persuade Hosna, who is unlikely to accept Wad Rayyes' proposal on his own.

Although such things are common in the village, the narrator is angry about the situation. He thinks that Wad Rayyes would be a cruel husband to Hosna, who is forty years his junior. He concludes that this marriage is just as immoral as Mustafa's cruelty to his English mistresses.

Analysis

In these chapters, Salih emphasizes the indifference of nature to the characters' experiences. This theme is explored through Mustafa's death in a flood, as well as the narrator's meditations about his grandfather. Although his grandfather seems to have a charmed, civilized existence, he is just as beholden to nature as anyone else is, and he could die in a disaster as easily as Mustafa Sa'eed did.

However, Salih complicates the narrator's argument that nature is omnipotent through these chapters' focus on the arrival of technology in Wad Hamid. The use of water pumps and pre-made doors seems to distance the villagers from nature. Salih seems to believe that this is a false sense of distance, though, and the villagers are really just as vulnerable as ever to the immutable force of the Nile, which can kill people as well as draw them upstream to Egypt and Europe. He is also critical of the changes that technology has made to daily life, putting Wad Baseer, one of the most skilled engineers in the village, out of work.

Wad Baseer is an autodidact who serves as a general village handyman; his career can be contrasted with that of the narrator, whose extensive education is highly specialized. For the narrator, the conditions of his labor are largely separate from its products—that is, he has an office job dedicated to education policy, but does not work directly with schools or children. This might explain why his policies are exposed as ineffectual later in the novel. Although the narrator means well, Salih endorses Wad Baseer's simple education and hands-on job as a better way to improve people's lives.

The discussion of female circumcision in Chapter 4 is extremely important. Bint Majzoub, the only woman in the group, appears to endorse female circumcision, but her position is complicated by the way she has lived her life. She greatly enjoys sex herself, but argues that female circumcision is good because it makes women unable to enjoy sex, and thus more focused on pleasing their lovers. This paradox suggests that Bint Majzoub may not be offering all of her opinions on the matter, and indeed she remains quiet throughout the rest of the conversation.

The discussion is also very important for understanding the character of Wad Rayyes. He appears to take the most progressive stance on the topic of circumcision, but his reasons for doing so are self-centered and borderline-misogynistic: he only opposes circumcision because he finds uncircumcised women more attractive. To emphasize the character's misogyny, the narrator adds that Wad Rayyes sees women only as interchangeable sex objects. The characterization in the discussion of circumcision helps explain the narrator's anger when he finds out that Wad Rayyes intends to marry Hosna.

Summary and Analysis of Chapter 6

Summary

The narrator goes to visit Hosna and her two sons. He had planned to visit anyway, since he is organizing the boys' circumcision ceremony, and he likes to check in and see how they are doing. The boys leave for school, and the narrator reflects that Hosna is a beautiful woman whom Wad Rayyes "wants to sacrifice at the edge of the grave, with which to bribe death and so gain a respite of a year or two" (75). The narrator has a long chat with Hosna and enjoys her company, but does not bring up Wad Rayyes's proposal.

The narrator asks Hosna if she loved Mustafa Sa'eed. She hesitates, and then replies tenderly that he was a generous husband and father. It becomes clear that she does not know about Mustafa's torrid past. However, she was suspicious because Mustafa would sometimes speak in "gibberish" (English) in his sleep. Hosna remembers that Mustafa put his affairs in order only a week before he died, and seemed to know that the end was near. She believes the answer to Mustafa's past is in his private room, to which she doesn't have the keys.

Hosna begins to cry, and the narrator wonders if he should hold her. He decides against it, and instead tells Hosna that she is still young and should move on with her life, and that she should maybe even accept one of the many suitors that want to marry her. She adamantly says that she will never remarry. The narrator reveals that Wad Rayyes has proposed, to which Hosna responds: "If they force me to marry, I'll kill him and kill myself" (80).

The next morning, Wad Rayyes asks how the narrator's intervention went. The narrator tells him that Hosna does not want to marry anyone, and he should forget the matter. Wad Rayyes gets teary-eyed, and seems genuinely upset, resolving, "She'll accept me whether she likes it or not ... She should thank God she's found a husband like me" (81). The narrator tries to reason with him, saying that there are plenty of other women in the village and Hosna refuses all of her suitors, so he shouldn't take it personally. Wad Rayyes becomes very angry that the narrator will not force Hosna to marry him, and resolves to marry her without the narrator's permission, since her father and brothers have already agreed to it.

The narrator goes to his old friend Mahjoub to ask for advice. Mahjoub believes that Wad Rayyes is "an old windbag" and will probably drop the issue, but even if he does not, the narrator can do nothing because Hosna's father and brothers already consented to the marriage. The narrator is saddened, as he believes that women should be make their own decisions about these matters. Mahjoub replies that the world has not changed as much as the narrator thinks it has, and men still own women, at least in Wad Hamid.

The conversation turns to Mustafa Sa'eed. Although Mahjoub initially did not like Mustafa, he was impressed by his work on the Agricultural Project Committee. Mustafa showed a great aptitude for accounting, and helped start a profitable flour mill and village store that provides fairly-priced supplies. The narrator continues to question Mahjoub about Mustafa, and Mahjoub wonders why the narrator is so obsessed with the man. Mahjoub also thinks it is strange that Mustafa made the narrator his executor, since the narrator is in Khartoum most of the time.

As the narrator prepares to leave, the two men go back to discussing Wad Rayyes. Mahjoub remains convinced that Wad Rayyes will soon turn his attention elsewhere. He then suggests that the narrator marry Hosna, since he is already the guardian of her children. The narrator becomes very nervous at this suggestion and tells Mahjoub that he is crazy. As he leaves, the narrator realizes he is in love with Hosna, and is "not immune from the germ of contagion which oozes from the body of the universe" (86)—sexual attraction.

Analysis

This chapter focuses the narrator's relationship with Hosna. Until now, she has only been alluded to and has not played a direct role in the story. Even after the narrator's long discussion with her at home, we do not learn much about her—most of Hosna's dialogue is paraphrased, and although we get a detailed description of her beauty, Salih does not delve far into her psyche. There is no explanation as to why she is so reluctant to remarry, and she is only quoted in the dialogue when she talks about Mustafa; the rest of her dialogue is summarized or paraphrased by the narrator.

As some critics have noted, the narrator sees Hosna as a tool to learn more about Mustafa Sa'eed (Davidson 392). This complicates his love for her. By this point in the text, it is clear that despite his assertions to the contrary, the narrator is completely preoccupied with learning as much as he can about Mustafa. Hosna, then, is a means to an end; the narrator will not only know everything about Mustafa, but he wishes to experience Mustafa's sex and family life firsthand.

The narrator's support for women's rights, then, is very convenient given his motives. Like Wad Rayyes, he is all in favor of women's rights when it will help him to get what he wants, but he still hesitates to intervene and stop the marriage. The narrator also has a curiously negative attitude toward sex, characterizing it as a "germ of contagion" that corrupted Mustafa and Wad Rayyes, and is now threatening to infect him as well. This creates a stark contrast to the rapturous portrayal of sex in the previous chapter, when Wad Rayyes and Bint Majzoub described their orgasms in detail.

However, unlike these village people, the narrator has traveled abroad, and like Mustafa Sa'eed, he continually associates sex with violence. The narrator sees sex as not just an interaction between individuals, but as an instrument for the systemic oppression of women. In both England and Sudan, premarital sex can tarnish a woman's reputation and destroy her emotionally (as evidenced by the suicides of Mustafa's mistresses). Men are not subject to these restrictions, and this freedom gives them power—power about which the narrator feels deeply conflicted, as evidenced by his reluctance to intervene in Hosna's marriage one way or the other.

This chapter also reveals more information about Mahjoub. Mahjoub was smart enough to pursue higher education, but chose to remain in the village and work directly with the people. He represents an alternative life path that the narrator could have taken. He also illustrates the fact that a British education, which is supposed to help the narrator make Sudan a better country, actually prevents him from doing so. Having taken a government job, the narrator does not interact directly with the people he is supposed to help. Furthermore, the narrator has become so progressive in his views that he is unable to help Hosna; by insisting that she should choose for herself, he overlooks the fact that she really has no choice, and the only way he can help her is by rejecting Wad Rayyes on her behalf.

Summary and Analysis of Chapters 7 and 8

Summary

After the boys' circumcision ceremony, the narrator decides to drive back to Khartoum, even though he usually takes a boat on the Nile. It is very hot driving through the desert, and delirious from the heat, the driver runs his truck into a dry riverbed. The narrator's mind wanders back to the events of his visit to Wad Hamid, and he dwells on bits of dialogue from the previous chapter.

The narrator thinks back to the circumcision ceremony, when he and Mahjoub got drunk and contemplated going into Mustafa's private room. However, they passed out before they could do so. He then fantasizes about Mustafa's sexual encounters with Isabella Seymour. The narrator imagines that Isabella worshipped Mustafa as a "black ... pagan god" (88-89), and that this conflicted with her religion, which is the real reason she killed herself.

The narrator and the driver continue their journey. When they pull over to rest, a Bedouin asks them for a cigarette. They give him one, and after smoking it, he has a seizure but recovers quickly. The narrator gives him the rest of his pack, and the truck continues on its way. He remains delirious from the heat, and quotes passages of Arabic poetry to himself. The truck passes a government car that has broken down, and the driver stops to give the soldiers some water and gasoline. The soldiers mention that they are on their way to arrest a tribal woman who killed her husband. They say that they do not know who the woman was, but the narrator does not believe them because it is so rare for a woman to kill a man. He suggests to the soldiers that the woman is innocent and the husband may have died of sunstroke. The soldiers and the narrator part ways.

The narrator resolves to write to Mrs. Robinson, who moved to the Isle of Wight after Mr. Robinson died of typhoid in Cairo. He believes that she can give him more information about Mustafa Sa'eed, since she was present at his trial. Night falls, and the truck stops overnight at a rest stop. The drivers sing and dance together, and a nearby Bedouin tribe joins the party.

Twenty-nine days later, the narrator receives a cable from Mahjoub saying that Hosna has murdered Wad Rayyes and killed herself, just as she promised. He immediately returns to Wad Hamid, and Mahjoub, who feels guilty about the tragedy, is the only person to greet him when he arrives. Although the narrator wants to know what happened, Mahjoub changes the subject and asks about the latest political developments in Khartoum. The narrator does not want to talk politics because he is ashamed at the behavior of the corrupt government officials. They spend millions of pounds on lavish clothing and offices while doing nothing to improve Sudanese schools.

Finally, Mahjoub explains to the narrator what happened with Hosna. Wad Rayyes continued to insist on the marriage, and Hosna's father beat her until she submitted. Furious at being forced into the marriage, she refused to have sex with Wad Rayyes or even speak to him. At this point, Mahjoub is interrupted by the narrator's mother, who is angry because she thinks that the narrator had an affair with Hosna. The narrator goes to visit his grandfather, who cries for Wad Rayyes but does not give him any new information.

The narrator goes to Bint Majzoub, reasoning that if she will not tell him what happened, no one will. She recalls hearing Hosna's screams one night, and assuming, along with the other villagers, that she has finally had sex with Wad Rayyes and is screaming from pleasure. Wad Rayyes eventually starts yelling too, and they realize he is calling for help. Bint Majzoub gets the men of the village, and they go to Wad Rayyes's house. They see that both Hosna and Wad Rayyes are naked. Hosna is covered in bits and scratches with a knife plunged into her heart, and Wad Rayyes has many stab wounds. Some of the women tried to hold a funeral for Hosna, but Mahjoub threatened to break their necks. Wad Rayyes's eldest wife, Mabrouka, is unfazed by his death, and she says he deserved it for forcing Hosna to marry him.

The narrator goes to see Mahjoub, who says that Hosna was insane and did not deserve a proper burial. The narrator is furious and attempts to strangle him. A scuffle ensues, and the narrator faints as he feels someone pulling him off Mahjoub.

Analysis

The short seventh chapter fits oddly into the rest of the narrative. None of its events is central to the plot, and Salih might easily have omitted it completely. Stylistically, it foreshadows the unification of Mustafa's and the narrator's consciousnesses in Chapter 9. It is initially implied that the narrator is alone on his journey back to Khartoum, and that he is driving the truck himself. We only learn that the driver is present when the narrator abruptly switches to the first-person plural ("we") halfway through the chapter. A similar transition will occur in Chapter 9, and again readers will have to infer who the other person is, rather than being told explicitly.

Chapter 7 also presents an unlikely parallel to the murder-suicide of Hosna and Wad Rayyes. The soldiers that the narrator encounters on the road cannot possibly be going to investigate the murder in Wad Hamid, since the narrator only finds out about the murder a month later, and even in Sudan, telegrams would not take four weeks to arrive. The narrator observes that it is exceptionally rare for women to murder their husbands, so this coincidence suggests that the murders are the result of some broader social discord.

The lyrical narration of Chapter 7 gives way to the narrator's more established, clear style in Chapter 8, when he returns to Wad Hamid after hearing of the murders. Bint Majzoub's assumption that Hosna's screams were from orgasms and not pain is significant because it reinforces Salih's association of sex with violence. For the women of Wad Hamid, the distinction between the two is blurred, because men use sex to subjugate and control women.

Given the violence and emotional power of Chapter 8, the narrator's digression about education policy stands out. Mahjoub argues that the narrator's latest project to unify African school curriculum is silly when schools are underfunded and children do not have the transportation to get to them. However, the real evil in this section is not the curriculum-unification plan, but rather the narrator's hypocritical colleagues, who spend government money on themselves and their wives. By placing this digression in the middle of the novel's most viscerally violent chapter, Salih associates the corruption with the viscerally violent description of the murder-suicide. Just as sex is a kind of violence used to control women, so corruption is a kind of violence used to control the Sudanese population, keeping them poor and uneducated.

Mahjoub's personality undergoes a surprising shift in this section. He has always seemed kind and levelheaded, but here he speaks very harshly of Hosna and denies her a funeral. This demonstrates the evolution of Mahjoub's character over the course of the novel, from a young socialist to a conservative village elder, who uses misogynistic language and threatens the village women with violence when they try to honor Hosna with a funeral. It also illustrates a key difference between Mahjoub and the narrator. Despite Mahjoub's political prowess, he is unable to accept real social change, whereas the narrator advocates for a truly liberal society, but is unable to act on his beliefs in an effective way. Together, the men represent opposite forms of hypocrisy. In this chapter, it becomes clear that their complementary skill sets come with drawbacks, and they can never work together to advance the country. The novel's early hope for Sudanese leadership is now tempered by pessimism.

Summary and Analysis of Chapters 9 and 10

Summary

The narrator switches from the past tense to the present. He says that his "adversary is within" (111), and that he is following Mustafa's example. Furious with hatred and desire for revenge, he goes to Mustafa Sa'eed's house and unlocks the private room. He lights a match and sees Mustafa Sa'eed, but it turns out to be the narrator's reflection in a mirror. He sees that the room is lavishly furnished, with Persian rugs, walls of books, and an oil painting of Jean Morris. The narrator thinks that keeping these remnants of European life is not proper behavior for "a man who wanted to turn over a new leaf" (112). He sets fire to one of the carpets, but then thinks better of it and stamps it out.

The narrator looks at Mustafa's books—mostly literature and economics texts, by English authors. He notices photographs of Sheila Greenwood, Isabella Seymour, and Ann Hammond, all of which have loving dedications to Mustafa written on them. The narrator thinks back to Mustafa's story, recalling his idyllic memories of Sheila. We also learn that Isabella's husband was a witness for the defense in Mustafa's trial. He testified that she had been diagnosed with cancer before she committed suicide. The narrator recalls Mustafa's story of meeting Ann Hammond. Mustafa had been giving a lecture about the poetry of Abu Nuwas, which he interpreted fancifully, with lots of fabricated information. Ann Hammond loves the lecture, and he buys her drinks and recites poetry for her. We also learn about a role-play that Mustafa would do with Ann Hammond, in which she pretended to be his "slave girl," Sausan.

Next the narrator sees a picture of Mustafa with Mr. and Mrs. Robinson. He remembers Mrs. Robinson's response to his letter, which he forgot about in the wake of the murder-suicide. Her letter had said that she pitied "Moozie," and that she forgives him for the murder. She hopes that Hosna and the children will come to visit her on the Isle of Wight, and she is writing a memoir about her life in Cairo with Mr. Robinson and Mustafa. Mrs. Robinson is the executor of Mustafa's affairs in London, and she has money that she wants the narrator to give to Hosna.

The narrator sees a newspaper from 1927. A long excerpt of the headlines from the newspaper follows, and the narrator wonders about its significance. He finds a notebook; its title page reads "My Life Story—by Mustafa Sa'eed" (125), but the rest of the pages are blank. There are many drawings of villagers in Mustafa's drawer, which show great skill. The person he drew most was Wad Rayyes; there are eight portraits of him. Again, the narrator wonders about the reason for this.

Beneath the drawings, the narrator finds some attempts at poetry and fiction. One of the poems is unfinished, and the narrator finishes it by writing the last line. He finds more scraps of paper on which Mustafa Sa'eed had written fragments about his life. The narrator speculates that Mustafa hid these scraps for the narrator to find and piece together. He judges this as egotistical and conceited, and resolves to burn the private room at dawn.

At last, the narrator turns his attention to the portrait of Jean Morris. He remembers what Mustafa said about her in more detail than appeared in Chapter 2. Jean Morris cruelly rejected him, until he turned his attention away from her. One night, she showed up at Mustafa's house and promised she would sleep with him if he gave her his possessions—a silk prayer mat, an antique manuscript, and a vase. One by one, she destroyed these items in front of Mustafa. When he tried to take her in his arms, she kicked him in the groin and left.

Eventually, Mustafa and Jean Morris married, and they would often get into violent fights. She would flirt with other men and insult Mustafa's masculinity, even in public. One cold evening, while they are having sex, Mustafa gently plunges a dagger into Jean's chest. She kisses it and accepts her murder with a kind of ecstasy, begging Mustafa to "come with me" (136).

The narrator decides that burning the private room will not do any good, and goes for a swim to help relieve his emotions. As he swims further and further into the Nile, he begins to feel himself drowning, and surrenders himself to that fate. However, he feels a sudden desire for a cigarette, and snaps out of his reverie, deciding that it is better to live. He reasons, "I shall live because there are a few people I want to stay with for the longest possible time and because I have duties to discharge" (139). He swims toward the shore and calls for help.

Analysis

The last two chapters resolve many questions about Mustafa's past. Through Mrs. Robinson's letter, we finally hear directly from one of the important women in Mustafa's life (even Hosna's dialogue is mostly paraphrased by the narrator or Bint Majzoub). Mustafa's early attraction to Mrs. Robinson influences his later relationships, and Salih borrows extensively from Freud's theories about psychosexual development as he develops Mrs. Robinson's character (Tarawneh and John, 331). She is a surrogate mother to Mustafa Sa'eed, and his great attraction to her (and indifference to his biological mother) foreshadows his turbulent relationships with English women. Mrs. Robinson's indulgent sentiments toward "Moozie" evoke the English mistresses' fascination with Mustafa as a representative of "Oriental" culture. He is simultaneously attracted to and resentful of this condescending attitude, and the fact that he experienced it as a child helps explain why.

The narrator waits until he enters Mustafa's private room to relate the most violent and sexually charged memories from Mustafa's story in Chapter 2. By adding pieces to Mustafa's story retroactively, the narrator undermines his own reliability; knowing that he has excised parts of the story in Chapter 2 invites questioning about what else he has excised from the story. It also enhances the mystique of the private room. None of the memories that we read about in Chapter 9 are actually new to the narrator; he has known about them since he was a young man. The private room is really just an ornate study. By waiting until the end of the novel to reveal the story of Jean Morris's murder, Salih endows the objects in the room with symbolism, and in doing so, confines Mustafa's story to that room—allowing the narrator to lock the door and move on with his life.

The memories of Jean Morris deserve particular scrutiny. Mustafa repeatedly emphasizes that Jean controlled Mustafa by destroying his possessions when they fought. However, Mustafa also emphasizes that these possessions—the Arabic books, the incense, the pottery—were mainly bought to enhance his persona as a wild African man from the East, which he used to seduce women. The fact that Jean Morris destroys these props suggests that she was the only one of Mustafa's lovers that related to him as a man, rather than as an African. Jean's insults are directed to Mustafa's masculinity; she does not talk much about his "Oriental" origins at all, especially compared to Ann, Sheila, and Isabella. This helps to explain why she arouses genuine violence and passion in Mustafa, and why he is unable to manipulate and discard her the way he did with the previous women.

At the beginning of Chapter 9, the narrator writes that "the adversary" is inside him, and he heads to Mustafa Sa'eed's private room to obtain vengeance. This seems counterintuitive, since one would assume that any vengeance would be wrought on Mahjoub, whom the narrator tried to strangle at the end of the previous chapter. Instead, the narrator blames his violence on the influence of Mustafa Sa'eed, and goes to the private room in an attempt to exorcise Mustafa's influence once and for all.

The narrator's choice not to drown himself in the Nile is a curious one. Such a death would evoke Mustafa's possible suicide, which the narrator characterizes as "a melodramatic act" earlier in the novel. Ultimately, the reasons that the narrator chooses to live are rather mundane—at first, he wants a cigarette, and then he decides that he wants to spend more time with the villagers and carry out his duties to Mustafa's sons. This choice of a simple, village-oriented existence is the ultimate rejection of the melodrama and violence of Mustafa's life. This choice is the narrator's only alternative to allowing his "migration to the North" to consume him, just as it did Mustafa. It seems that he has finally found the "middle way" discussed on page 89.

Suggested Essay Questions

1. **Discuss Bint Majzoub in relation to Salih's broader portrayal of women. How does Bint Majzoub subvert her society's expectations of what women can do? How does she uphold them?**

   Bint Majzoub is an assertive, outspoken woman who rebels against social conventions by drinking and hanging around with men. However, her rebellion is problematic, and she does not present a viable alternative to Wad Hamid's oppression of women. For example, she is famous for being outspoken about sex, but she talks about it in graphic, misogynistic language, and she believes that women should prioritize their husband's sexual pleasure above their own. Furthermore, she is able to flout social convention largely because she is a widow and independently wealthy, but she inherited this money from her husbands, rather than earning it herself.
2. **Season of Migration to the North depicts many kinds of political participation. What obligations does Salih suggest the individual has to his / her country?**

   Mustafa Sa'eed and Mahjoub both talk about the obligation that educated people have to help make the fledgling independent nation of Sudan a better place. The narrator tries to do this by working for the Ministry of Education, but he is ineffective because he is content to work in his office and does not speak out about the rampant corruption among his coworkers. In contrast, Mahjoub helps people directly by spearheading the Agricultural Project Committee and later becoming the leader of the village. Through these different portraits of national service, Salih suggests that the best way to serve one's country is to speak out against injustice and be active in one's own community.
3. **Mustafa Sa'eed has three girlfriends and two wives over the course of the novel. Compare and contrast his relationships with women. Do his relationships mature as he gets older?**

   Mustafa realizes early on that exaggerating the "Eastern" elements of his personality attracts attention from English women. Each of his English mistresses is fascinated with "Oriental" culture, and they love Mustafa for being a representative of this culture—they do not see him as a human being. In contrast, Jean Morris and Hosna bint Mahmoud connect with Mustafa on a deeper level. Jean Morris brings out his violent side, and takes little notice of the African knickknacks with which Mustafa decorates his home. She even destroys some of them, objects that are symbolic of Mustafa's deception of his earlier lovers. Meanwhile, Hosna bint Mahmoud obviously does not see Mustafa as a representative of any particular culture, and only desires a quiet village life. Nevertheless, although Mustafa seems to develop a preference for deeper women over the course of the novel, he remains self-centered—ultimately Hosna is only the means by which he achieves the simple village life for which he longs.

4. **The interlude when the narrator returns to Khartoum by truck (Chapter 7) is not clearly related to the rest of the plot. What might be its importance to the novel?**

   In this mystical, atmospheric interlude, Salih foregrounds the narrator's stream of consciousness. Usually the narrator is a lucid, concise storyteller that remains guarded about his own feelings, but here we see the truly obsessive nature of his thoughts about Hosna and Mustafa. This chapter also contains numerous instances of foreshadowing: the tribal woman that murders her husband, and the Bedouin who wants a cigarette more than water, even though he risks dying of thirst. By foreshadowing Hosna's murder-suicide and the narrator's decision not to kill himself in Chapter 10, Salih suggests that these dramatic experiences are not exclusive to his characters, but are rather could happen to anyone living in similar conditions.

5. **What is the significance of the narrator's choice not to intervene in Hosna's marriage to Wad Rayyes?**

   The narrator is so uncomfortable making decisions for Hosna that he refuses to intervene in her marriage, even when *not* intervening means that she will be forced to marry someone she hates. This represents the paradox of being a liberal in the highly conservative society of Wad Hamid—in order to actually improve people's lives through his enlightened principles, the narrator must behave in a way that contradicts these selfsame principles. The marriage dilemma is comparable to the narrator's inability to speak out about the fact that his fellow government workers are corrupt and inefficient.

6. **Mustafa and the narrator are the only characters who have been to Europe. Compare and contrast their reactions to traveling abroad.**

   For Mustafa Sa'eed, visiting Europe allows him to abandon the social constraints of African society, and he takes advantage of this, living a promiscuous lifestyle and blatantly fabricating his lectures. It seems that European society has made him corrupt, but in fact, Mustafa was immoral even when he lived in Sudan and Cairo; he acknowledges that he never cared about anyone but himself. English society simply allows him more leeway to put his solipsistic worldview into practice. The narrator has better intentions, and while he is coy about his love life in Europe, he seems to have focused more on academics. Traveling teaches the narrator to think critically, but it is unclear whether this skill is useful. Arguably, his tendency to over-think prevents him from intervening in Hosna's marriage and in the government corruption around him.

7. **Salih makes a point of explaining the political views of both the prosecuting and the defense attorney in Mustafa Sa'eed's trial. Why**

might this information be salient? And what is the significance of the fact that the prosecutor is a liberal and the defense attorney is a conservative?

In England at this time, a person's political affiliation often determined their attitudes toward foreigners, with liberals being stereotyped as more accepting of other cultures. By making the defense attorney a conservative and the prosecutor a liberal, Salih undercuts this simplistic stereotyping. He emphasizes that although the lawyers try to turn Mustafa's trial into a grand political narrative, they are both focused primarily on themselves. Their self-interest is ultimately more important to them than politics or their personal relationship to Mustafa, and Salih seems to imply that this is human nature and can be generalized to anyone.

8. **Explain the significance of the narrator's preoccupation with Mustafa Sa'eed. What does it reveal about his character?**

   The narrator is preoccupied with Mustafa because he recognizes parallels to his own experience and feelings in the older man's life story. Mustafa responds violently to the pressures of living in English society, and the narrator sees this as an alternative path that he might have taken himself. The question of whether the narrator is really so similar to Mustafa is resolved when the narrator becomes his executor, and is forced to deal with the aftermath of Mustafa's turbulent past.

9. ***Season of Migration to the North* includes at least four suicides. Discuss the relationship between suicide and character development in the novel.**

   The narrator characterizes Mustafa's possible suicide as a "melodramatic act." This can be extrapolated to the other characters' suicides as well. Ann Hammond, Sheila Greenwood, Isabella Seymour all kill themselves because Mustafa refuses to marry them. In doing so, they immortalize themselves in his memory; the book mentions that Mustafa had other mistresses, but they are not described or named because they did not kill themselves. Hosna bint Mahmoud's suicide is similar; it is incredibly loud and gruesome, and it seems that she not only wants to kill Wad Rayyes but express her anger at being forced to marry him in the first place. The novel's female characters use suicide not only to escape seemingly insoluble problems, but also to resolve these problems through the "melodramatic act."

10. **Analyze the argument about female circumcision. How do the opinions of Wad Rayyes, Bakri, and Bint Majzoub inform their characterization? What is the conversation's broader thematic significance?**

    The circumcision conversation reveals nuances to these characters that will be expanded upon later in the novel. Despite his apparent love for Hosna, Wad Rayyes is fundamentally self-centered, and despite her initial characterization as a liberated woman, Bint Majzoub has internalized her society's misogynistic attitudes. Bakri seems like he will be a moderating force and could convince Wad Rayyes to give up the marriage proposal, but he ultimately decides not to intervene, a choice that is foreshadowed by his apathy on the topic of circumcision. The conversation reflects the novel's broader theme that of pervasive misogyny in village culture.

Sudanese Independence: Before and After

For most of its history, the region of Sudan has not been a unified country. Spanning over nearly one million square miles, the region is mostly desert, bisected by a narrow fertile strip on either side of the Nile. It was historically inhabited by a wide variety of tribes, kingdoms, and principalities. The northern part of the country was forcefully unified in 1820-1821, when Egypt annexed the area. Several other attempts were made to unify Sudan, but they met with limited success. Finally, Great Britain and Egypt formed an alliance to invade the country. They succeeded, unifying the entire area that is today known as Sudan, under a predominantly British government.

After the Second World War, Great Britain's economy and military were devastated. Recognizing that many African countries were beginning to rebel against their European governments, the British signed a treaty with Egypt that would grant Sudan independence in 1953, with the region officially gaining "home rule" starting on January 1, 1956. During the transitional period between 1953 and 1956, a constitution was drafted, but it was vague about a number of important issues, including the role of the military in government, the separation of mosque and state, and whether the government would be federal or unitary. This laid the groundwork for intense strife between the predominantly Muslim, Arab northern region of Sudan, and the mainly Christian and animist south, populated mostly by ethnic Africans. Civil war broke out before the country had even received its official independence.

An inefficient and corrupt government also plagued the fledgling nation. This undermined even the dictatorship's good-faith efforts to establish schools in rural areas, a problem that Salih portrays in *Season of Migration to the North*. From 1958 to 1964, the country was ruled by General Ibrahim Abboud, who suspended the constitution and intervened heavily in the economy, all while enacting policies of Islamification. However, he was unable to control the country due to increasing rebellions in the south, and was succeeded by a series of short-lived, impotent rulers. It was in this period that Salih wrote the novel while living abroad.

Since 1969, Sudan has been controlled by a series of dictators, most of whom have enforced strict Islamist policies. The civil war persisted on and off until 2002, with scattered violence remaining. A referendum for southern independence was held in January 2011, with the south voting overwhelmingly to secede. The country has also received attention and infamy as the site of the Darfur genocide, a separate conflict that has been ongoing in the southwestern region since 2003 and cost more than 400,000 lives.

Author of ClassicNote and Sources

Abigail Lind, author of ClassicNote. Completed on May 27, 2011, copyright held by GradeSaver.

Updated and revised Bella Wang May 31, 2011. Copyright held by GradeSaver.

Tayeb Salih, introduction by Laila Lalami. Season of Migration to the North. New York: NYRB Classics, 2009.

Central Intelligence Agency. "The World Factbook: Sudan." The CIA World Factbook. 2011-05-23. 2011-05-27. <https://www.cia.gov/library/publications/the-world-factbook/geos/su.html>.

U.S. Department of State. "Background Note: Sudan." Bureau of African Affairs. 2011-04-08. 2011-05-27. <http://www.state.gov/r/pa/ei/bgn/5424.htm>.

Jamal Mahjoub. "Tayeb Salih." The Guardian. 2009-02-20. 2011-05-27. <http://www.guardian.co.uk/books/2009/feb/20/obituary-tayeb-salih>.

John Lingan. "'Season of Migration to the North' by Tayeb Salih." The Quarterly Conversation. 2009-04-21. 2011-05-27. <http://quarterlyconversation.com/season-of-migration-to-the-north-by-tayeb-salih-review>.

Marina Harss. "Season of Migration to the North." Words Without Borders.. 2007-01-01. 2011-05-27. <http://wordswithoutborders.org/book-review/season-of-migration-to-the-north/>.

Maud Newton. "After the Colonizers Depart." National Public Radio. 2009-05-18. 2011-05-27. <http://www.npr.org/templates/story/story.php?storyId=104205048>.

John E. Davidson. "In Search of a Middle Point: The Origins of Oppression in Tayeb Salih's 'Season of Migration to the North.'" *Research in African Literatures* 20.3 (Autumn 1989), pp. 385-400.

Yosif Tarawneh and Joseph John. "Tayeb Salih and Freud: The Impact of Freudian Ideas on 'Season of Migration to the North.'" *Arabica* 35.3 (Nov. 1988), p. 328-349.

Quiz 1

1. **Where was the narrator's favorite place to play as a child?**
   A. His family's I[diwan] (reception room)
   B. His grandfather's house
   C. The acacia tree by the Nile
   D. The village square

2. **How long did the narrator study in England?**
   A. Two years
   B. Four years
   C. Seven years
   D. One semester

3. **What kind of fruit does Mustafa bring when he introduces himself to the narrator?**
   A. Berries
   B. Watermelon and oranges
   C. Peaches and pears
   D. Apples and bananas

4. **After finding out that the narrator has a doctorate in English poetry, Mustafa remarks that a more practical discipline would be more useful to the country. Which of these subjects does he NOT suggest as a better choice for the narrator?**
   A. Medicine
   B. Diplomacy
   C. Engineering
   D. Agriculture

5. **What famous anti-war poem does Mustafa Sa'eed recite that arouses the narrator's suspicion?**
   A. "Dulce et Decorum Est" by Wilfred Owen
   B. "MCMXIV" by Philip Larkin
   C. "Antwerp" by Ford Madox Hueffer
   D. "How to Die" by Siegfried Sassoon

6. **On what condition does Mustafa Sa'eed promise to tell the narrator his life story?**
   A. Total secrecy
   B. The narrator's fortune
   C. That the narrator will be his executor when he dies
   D. That the narrator will not tell Hosna

7. **Where was Mustafa Sa'eed born?**
   A. London
   B. Wad Hamid
   C. Khartoum
   D. Cairo

8. **When the narrator first returns from England, what does Mahjoub ask him?**
   A. Whether there are farmers in Europe
   B. If it's true that the British live in sin without getting married
   C. What Europeans do when it snows in the winter
   D. Whether British women are circumcised

9. **When the narrator was homesick while studying in England, whom did he dream of?**
   A. His grandfather
   B. His father
   C. Hosna bint Mahmoud
   D. Bint Majzoub

10. **Who is the president of the Agricultural Project Committee?**
   A. Mustafa Sa'eed
   B. The narrator's father
   C. Mahmoud
   D. The narrator

11. **Why does Mustafa Sa'eed want to go to school as a boy?**
   A. He wants to make money to support his mother
   B. Because he is in love with the social worker who is enrolling children in school
   C. Because he wants to study abroad
   D. Because he likes the hat of the social worker who is enrolling children in school

12. **After enrolling in school, how long does it take Mustafa to learn to write?**
   A. One week
   B. One year
   C. Two weeks
   D. Three months

13. **When describing his time in school, Mustafa repeatedly compares his mind to what object?**
    A. A mirror
    B. The thirsty Sahara
    C. A sharp knife
    D. A shiny razor

14. **How old is Mustafa when he goes to high school in Cairo?**
    A. Twelve
    B. Fifteen
    C. Fourteen
    D. Eight

15. **What is the name of the headmaster of Mustafa's elementary school?**
    A. Mahmoud Effendi
    B. Professor Maxwell Foster-Keen
    C. Mr. Robinson
    D. Mr. Stockwell

16. **Fill in the blank of this repeated refrain: "And the train carried me to Victoria Station and to the world of _____________."**
    A. Oxford
    B. Ann Hammond
    C. Jean Morris
    D. women

17. **How does Mustafa meet Jean Morris?**
    A. At a party
    B. At a book signing
    C. Through a classified ad
    D. At a lecture

18. **What pseudonym does Mustafa use with Isabella Seymour?**
    A. Abdul Asad
    B. Amin Hassan
    C. Wazir Miyaz
    D. Ismail Nadir

19. **In Chapter 1, Mustafa says to the narrator, "Your grandfather knows the secret." What is the secret?**
    A. Where the key to Mustafa's private room is.
    B. That simplicity is the key to a happy life.
    C. That a loving marriage is the key to a happy life.
    D. That faith in God is the key to a happy life.

20. **Which of Mustafa's lovers is married when they have their affair?**
    A. Sheila Greenwood
    B. Isabella Seymour
    C. Ann Hammond
    D. Jean Morris

21. **When they cannot find Mustafa Sa'eed's body after the flood, what do the villagers assume happened to him?**
    A. He killed himself
    B. He is hiding in the village
    C. He was eaten by crocodiles
    D. He ran off with Bint Majzoub

22. **What was Mustafa Sa'eed's nickname in elementary school?**
    A. The black Englishman
    B. The brilliant beggar
    C. The police-in-training
    D. Four-Eyes

23. **What is the Mamur's main complaint about the British rule of Sudan?**
    A. That the civil servants were all corrupt
    B. That the British forced the local population into slave labor
    C. That the education system was inefficient
    D. That the best government jobs were given to "nobodies"

24. **Before working for the government, which subject did the narrator teach in secondary schools?**
    A. Modern Arabic poetry
    B. Writing
    C. English poetry
    D. Pre-Islamic poetry

25. **What accusation does Richard make about Mustafa's academic work?**
   A. That he plagiarized it
   B. That he fudged his statistics
   C. That he wrote badly
   D. That he cherry-picked his sources

Quiz 1 Answer Key

1. **(C)** The acacia tree by the Nile
2. **(C)** Seven years
3. **(B)** Watermelon and oranges
4. **(B)** Diplomacy
5. **(C)** "Antwerp" by Ford Madox Hueffer
6. **(A)** Total secrecy
7. **(C)** Khartoum
8. **(A)** Whether there are farmers in Europe
9. **(A)** His grandfather
10. **(C)** Mahmoud
11. **(D)** Because he likes the hat of the social worker who is enrolling children in school
12. **(C)** Two weeks
13. **(C)** A sharp knife
14. **(A)** Twelve
15. **(D)** Mr. Stockwell
16. **(C)** Jean Morris
17. **(A)** At a party
18. **(B)** Amin Hassan
19. **(B)** That simplicity is the key to a happy life.
20. **(B)** Isabella Seymour
21. **(C)** He was eaten by crocodiles
22. **(A)** The black Englishman
23. **(D)** That the best government jobs were given to "nobodies"
24. **(D)** Pre-Islamic poetry
25. **(B)** That he fudged his statistics

Quiz 2

1. **When the narrator overhears Wad Rayyes having sex with his wife, how does he react?**
    A. He is sad because he cannot find anyone to have sex with himself
    B. He is nervous that other villagers will also hear
    C. He is angry that Wad Rayyes wishes to violate Hosna in a similar way
    D. He is ashamed for hearing something he shouldn't have

2. **For which government ministry does the narrator work?**
    A. The Ministry of Agriculture
    B. The Ministry of Finance
    C. The Ministry of Justice
    D. The Ministry of Education

3. **At which important diplomatic event was Mustafa Sa'eed rumored to have been a secretary?**
    A. The Sudanese Independence Conference of 1956
    B. The Paris Peace Conference of 1947
    C. The Munich Conference of 1938
    D. The British Naval Conference of 1936

4. **What unfinished building does the narrator observe when he returns to Wad Hamid on vacation?**
    A. A school
    B. A grocery store
    C. A hospital
    D. A post office

5. **What alternative explanation does Ann Hammond's father suggest for her suicide?**
    A. She was failing out of Oxford
    B. She had discovered she was pregnant
    C. She couldn't find a job after graduating from Oxford
    D. She was trying to choose a religion and was suffering a spritual crisis

6. **What is Mustafa's sentence for murdering Jean Morris?**
    A. Life in prison
    B. Seven years in prison
    C. Twenty years in prison
    D. Capital punishment

7. **What is the narrator's grandfather's most prized possession?**
   A. His prayer mat
   B. His prayer beads
   C. His wedding ring
   D. His chickens

8. **After Wad Rayyes rapes a slave girl in his youth, how does the village respond?**
   A. They force him to marry his cousin
   B. They banish him
   C. They sell the slave girl to another village, and don't punish Wad Rayyes
   D. They force him to marry the slave girl

9. **How many husbands did Bint Majzoub have in her lifetime?**
   A. One
   B. Five
   C. Eight
   D. Three

10. **When Bint Majzoub's daughter marries a husband of whom her mother disapproves, how does Bint Majzoub get rid of him?**
   A. She poisons him
   B. She implies that he cannot satisfy her daughter sexually
   C. She encourages her daughter to have an affair
   D. She complains that he is too poor

11. **Why does Wad Rayyes wear kohl on his face?**
   A. He says it is commanded by Muslim law
   B. He is in disguise
   C. He wants to impress Hosna bint Mahmoud
   D. He wants to look handsome

12. **Why does Bint Majzoub seem to support female circumcision?**
   A. She thinks it makes the female genitalia look more attractive
   B. She is circumcised herself, and wants every woman to experience what she did
   C. It prevents women from behaving immorally
   D. She thinks it makes women work harder to please their lovers

13. **What is Bakri's opinion of female circumcision?**

A. He thinks that all women should undergo it.

B. He doesn't think it matters either way.

C. He thinks it should be outlawed.

D. He is personally against it, but believes the choice should be left to womens' families.

14. **What do Wad Rayyes, Bakri, Bint Majzoub, and the narrator's grandfather do after joking together about sex?**

A. Go home

B. Swear each other to secrecy

C. Pray for forgiveness

D. Have dinner

15. **Why does Wad Rayyes invite the narrator to lunch?**

A. To discuss their political differences

B. To ask his permission to marry Hosna bint Mahmoud

C. To hear more about his time in England

D. To play backgammon

16. **Why does the narrator's grandfather approve of Wad Rayyes marrying Hosna?**

A. Wad Rayyes is rich and still very healthy for his age

B. Wad Rayyes' reputation as a womanizer is inaccurate

C. Hosna is having trouble raising her sons by herself

D. Wad Rayyes is lonely and Hosna will cheer him up

17. **Why did the narrator's grandfather travel to Egypt in his youth?**

A. To study in Cairo

B. To see the pyramids

C. As part of his pilgrimage to Mecca

D. To find a wife

18. **What is Wad Rayyes's main reason for opposing female circumcision?**

A. Circumcision is not called for in the Koran

B. Circumcision is painful and prevents women from enjoying sex

C. Uncircumcised women are more fun to have sex with

D. The circumcision process is gruesome

19. **What is the real name of the narrator's grandfather?**
   A. Hajj Ahmed
   B. Wad Rayyes
   C. Wad Basheer
   D. Abdul Karim

20. **Who was Bint Majzoub's favorite husband?**
   A. The narrator's grandfather
   B. Sa'eed the shopkeeper
   C. Wad Baseer
   D. Wad Basheer

21. **Why is the narrator angry when Wad Rayyes asks his permission to marry Hosna?**
   A. He believes Wad Rayyes is impotent
   B. He believes that Hosna should decide for herself
   C. He was trying to match Hosna with Mahmoud
   D. He believes Wad Rayyes is too poor for her

22. **What is the age difference between Hosna Bint Mahmoud and Wad Rayyes?**
   A. Three years
   B. Forty years
   C. Sixty years
   D. Twenty years

23. **What does Mustafa Sa'eed want for his sons?**
   A. Enough money to live comfortably
   B. An education in a religious school
   C. A normal upbringing and a worthwhile career
   D. Opportunities to travel

24. **What are the names of Hosna and Mustafa's children?**
   A. Zein and Majzoub
   B. Mahmoud and Sa'eed
   C. Mahjoub and Zahra
   D. Suleyman and Ahmed

25. **Mustafa Sa'eed asks the narrator to spare his sons "the pangs of wanderlust." What does the narrator do in response to this?**
   A. He decides that the boys can travel as adults if they want to
   B. He tells the boys scary stories about England
   C. He prohibits the boys from leaving the village
   D. He hides the boys' inheritance so they have no money to travel

Quiz 2 Answer Key

1. **(D)** He is ashamed for hearing something he shouldn't have
2. **(D)** The Ministry of Education
3. **(D)** The British Naval Conference of 1936
4. **(C)** A hospital
5. **(D)** She was trying to choose a religion and was suffering a spritual crisis
6. **(B)** Seven years in prison
7. **(B)** His prayer beads
8. **(A)** They force him to marry his cousin
9. **(B)** Five
10. **(B)** She implies that he cannot satisfy her daughter sexually
11. **(A)** He says it is commanded by Muslim law
12. **(A)** She thinks it makes the female genitalia look more attractive
13. **(B)** He doesn't think it matters either way.
14. **(C)** Pray for forgiveness
15. **(B)** To ask his permission to marry Hosna bint Mahmoud
16. **(A)** Wad Rayyes is rich and still very healthy for his age
17. **(C)** As part of his pilgrimage to Mecca
18. **(C)** Uncircumcised women are more fun to have sex with
19. **(A)** Hajj Ahmed
20. **(D)** Wad Basheer
21. **(B)** He believes that Hosna should decide for herself
22. **(B)** Forty years
23. **(C)** A normal upbringing and a worthwhile career
24. **(B)** Mahmoud and Sa'eed
25. **(A)** He decides that the boys can travel as adults if they want to

Quiz 3

1. **What event does the narrator organize for Mustafa Sa'eed's sons?**
   A. Their birthday party
   B. Their weddings
   C. Their circumcision ceremony
   D. Their graduation party

2. **Why did Hosna believe Mustafa Sa'eed was hiding something about his past?**
   A. He kept pictures of English women in their bedroom
   B. He spoke in English in his sleep
   C. He would disappear for several weeks at a time
   D. He wouldn't let her go in his private room

3. **Which political party does Mahjoub belong to?**
   A. The Democratic Unionist Party
   B. The People's Liberation Movement
   C. The Communist Party
   D. The National Democratic Socialist Party

4. **How does Mahjoub know Mustafa Sa'eed?**
   A. Mahjoub's daughter is betrothed to one of Mustafa's sons
   B. They went to school together
   C. They are both on the Agricultural Project Committee
   D. They are neighbors

5. **Which of these was NOT one of Mustafa's projects on the Agricultural Project Committee?**
   A. Starting a flour mill
   B. Distributing pesticides to farmers
   C. Starting a cooperative supply store
   D. Organizing the accounts

6. **Why does Mahjoub think it's strange that Mustafa made the narrator his executor?**
   A. Mustafa and the narrator did not get along
   B. The narrator is thought of as a troublemaker in Wad Hamid
   C. The narrator is in Khartoum most of the year
   D. The narrator is in love with Hosna

7. **Why does Mahjoub suggest that the narrator marry Hosna?**
   A. Because Hosna is destitute
   B. Because he is getting old and ought to settle down
   C. Because he is already the guardian of her children
   D. Because he is clearly in love with her

8. **How much education does Mahjoub have?**
   A. A doctorate
   B. A bachelor's degree
   C. High school
   D. Elementary school

9. **How does the narrator usually get from Khartoum to Wad Hamid?**
   A. By boat
   B. On foot
   C. By camel
   D. By truck

10. **What does the Bedouin trick the narrator's uncle, Abdul Karim, into buying?**
    A. A black donkey
    B. An elderly slave
    C. Diluted arak
    D. A white horse

11. **What does Mahjoub think Mustafa keeps in his private room?**
    A. Alcohol
    B. Treasure
    C. Dead bodies
    D. A second wife

12. **What does the Bedouin ask the narrator for on his way to Khartoum?**
    A. Gasoline
    B. A cigarette
    C. Water
    D. Money

13. **What alternative explanation does the narrator suggest for the El-Mirisab woman's murder of her husband?**
    A. He committed suicide
    B. He was terminally ill
    C. He assaulted her and she accidentally killed him in self-defense
    D. He died of sunstroke

14. **Where does Mrs. Robinson live in the 'present-day' section of the novel?**
    A. London
    B. Surrey
    C. The Isle of Wight
    D. Cairo

15. **How does Mr. Robinson die?**
    A. He is murdered
    B. Typhoid
    C. Sunstroke
    D. He commits suicide

16. **What is the goal of the education conference that the narrator attends in Khartoum?**
    A. To enroll more rural children
    B. To decide on the content of history textbooks
    C. To unify school curriculum throughout Africa
    D. To raise more funding for schools

17. **Who does Hosna ask to marry instead of Wad Rayyes?**
    A. The narrator's father
    B. Mahjoub
    C. Bakri
    D. The narrator

18. **Why does the narrator's mother get angry at him?**
    A. He takes a job in Khartoum instead of staying in Wad Hamid
    B. She thinks he had an affair with Hosna
    C. He studied abroad
    D. He refuses to get married

19. **Who attends the wedding of Hosna and Wad Rayyes?**
    A. Only Wad Rayyes's friends
    B. Only the narrator
    C. No one
    D. Only the couple's families

20. **What gift does the narrator give to Bint Majzoub?**
    A. Tobacco
    B. Whiskey
    C. Lingerie
    D. Part of Mustafa's estate

21. **When the villagers first hear Hosna's screams on the night she kills Wad Rayyes, why do they think she is screaming?**
    A. She is having an orgasm
    B. She misses Mustafa
    C. She burned herself while cooking
    D. She wants to have sex but Wad Rayyes is impotent

22. **How does Hosna kill Wad Rayyes?**
    A. She shoots him
    B. She stabs him to death
    C. She poisons him
    D. She pushes him down a well

23. **How does Wad Rayyes's eldest wife, Mabrouka, react to his death?**
    A. She is distraught and begins to pray
    B. She is pleased and holds a celebration
    C. She kills herself
    D. She is indifferent and goes back to sleep

24. **How does the narrator find out about the murder-suicide?**
    A. His grandfather sends a messenger
    B. By phone call from his mother
    C. By a letter Hosna sent before she did it
    D. By telegram from Mahjoub

25. **Why does Hosna's father insist that she marry Wad Rayyes?**

A. Wad Rayyes is rich and the family needs the money

B. He does not want Hosna to marry the narrator

C. He will be humiliated if Hosna doesn't obey him

D. He does not believe Hosna can raise two sons by herself

Quiz 3 Answer Key

1. **(C)** Their circumcision ceremony
2. **(B)** He spoke in English in his sleep
3. **(D)** The National Democratic Socialist Party
4. **(C)** They are both on the Agricultural Project Committee
5. **(B)** Distributing pesticides to farmers
6. **(C)** The narrator is in Khartoum most of the year
7. **(C)** Because he is already the guardian of her children
8. **(D)** Elementary school
9. **(A)** By boat
10. **(A)** A black donkey
11. **(B)** Treasure
12. **(B)** A cigarette
13. **(D)** He died of sunstroke
14. **(C)** The Isle of Wight
15. **(B)** Typhoid
16. **(C)** To unify school curriculum throughout Africa
17. **(D)** The narrator
18. **(B)** She thinks he had an affair with Hosna
19. **(A)** Only Wad Rayyes's friends
20. **(B)** Whiskey
21. **(A)** She is having an orgasm
22. **(B)** She stabs him to death
23. **(D)** She is indifferent and goes back to sleep
24. **(D)** By telegram from Mahjoub
25. **(C)** He will be humiliated if Hosna doesn't obey him

Quiz 4

1. **What does Mahjoub say that provokes the narrator to try to kill him?**
   A. That Wad Rayyes and Hosna made a good couple
   B. That he is in love with the narrator's mother
   C. That he, too, is in love with Hosna
   D. That Hosna didn't deserve a proper burial

2. **What body part does Wad Rayyes bite off when he is trying to defend himself against Hosna?**
   A. Her finger
   B. Her nipple
   C. Her earlobe
   D. Her lower lip

3. **Who painted the portrait of Jean Morris in Mustafa's private room?**
   A. Mustafa
   B. Jean Morris
   C. Andrew Wyeth
   D. The narrator

4. **What does the narrator burn in Mustafa's private room?**
   A. The portrait of Jean Morris
   B. The photos of Ann Hammond, Sheila Greenwood, and Isabella Seymour
   C. The books
   D. A rug

5. **What kind of books does Mustafa keep in his private room?**
   A. Arabic poetry
   B. Banned erotic novels
   C. Banned political pamphlets
   D. Books in English

6. **What is Mustafa Sa'eed's academic speciality?**
   A. Gender Studies
   B. Economics
   C. Political Science
   D. Literature

7. **What is Ann Hammond's "slave name?"**
   A. Zahira
   B. Batool
   C. Sausan
   D. Sabah

8. **What role does Isabella Seymour's husband play in Mustafa's trial?**
   A. Witness for the prosecution
   B. Witness for the defense
   C. Chief prosecutor
   D. Juror

9. **What alternative explanation does Isabella Seymour's husband give for her suicide?**
   A. She had cancer
   B. She was pregnant
   C. They had no money
   D. He was going to divorce her

10. **What is Ann Hammond wearing in the photograph that Mustafa keeps in his private room?**
    A. A mortarboard and graduation gown
    B. Nothing
    C. A revealing nightgown
    D. An Arab robe

11. **Which of Mustafa's English lovers speaks Arabic?**
    A. Sheila Greenwood
    B. Isabella Seymour
    C. Ann Hammond
    D. Jean Morris

12. **Which poet does Mustafa quote to Ann Hammond?**
    A. Abu Nuwas
    B. Ibrahim Ali Salman
    C. Omar Khayyam
    D. Thomas Hardy

13. **What is Mrs. Robinson's nickname for Mustafa?**
   A. Moozie
   B. Hot 'Staf
   C. Blossom
   D. Little Omar Khayyam

14. **Who was Mustafa Sa'eed's favorite person to draw?**
   A. Wad Rayyes
   B. Jean Morris
   C. Hosna bint Mahmoud
   D. The narrator

15. **Why does the narrator choose not to drown?**
   A. The water is too cold
   B. It is too painful
   C. He is frightened by the crocodiles in the water
   D. He wants a cigarette

16. **Which university does Mustafa study at?**
   A. Oxford
   B. Harvard
   C. Cambridge
   D. Leeds

17. **What does Mrs. Robinson ask the narrator to mail her?**
   A. A photo of Hosna and her sons
   B. Her share of Mustafa's estate
   C. A map of Wad Hamid
   D. A photo of himself

18. **Which of Mustafa's lovers is from the working class?**
   A. Sheila Greenwood
   B. Isabella Seymour
   C. Ann Hammond
   D. Jean Morris

19. **Which of these items does Jean Morris NOT destroy when she is seducing Mustafa?**
    A. His antique scrolls
    B. A wine glass
    C. A prayer mat
    D. A vase

20. **Who accuses the narrator of being preoccupied with Mustafa?**
    A. Mahjoub
    B. His grandfather
    C. His mother
    D. Hosna

21. **What tragedy immediatelv precedes Hosna's murder of Wad Rayyes?**
    A. An earthquake
    B. A tribal woman murders her husband
    C. Some children drown in the Nile
    D. A wildfire destroys the village

22. **Why is the narrator embarrassed to discuss politics with Mahjoub?**
    A. Mahjoub teases him about his support for women's rights
    B. He is not as knowledgeable as Mahjoub
    C. He has quit his government job but has not told anyone yet
    D. His fellow government employees are corrupt

23. **Why doesn't the narrator burn Mustafa's private room?**
    A. Because doing so won't solve his problems
    B. Because he is afraid it will spread to the rest of the house
    C. Because he has no matches
    D. Because the furniture inside is too valuable

24. **How old is Mustafa when he becomes a lecturer?**
    A. Thirty
    B. Sixteen
    C. Twenty-two
    D. Twenty-four

25. **Among Mustafa's things, the narrator discovers an unfinished poem. What does he do with it?**

A. He burns it

B. He copies it and tells Hosna he wrote it himself

C. He finishes the last lines

D. He gets it published

Quiz 4 Answer Key

1. **(D)** That Hosna didn't deserve a proper burial
2. **(B)** Her nipple
3. **(A)** Mustafa
4. **(D)** A rug
5. **(D)** Books in English
6. **(B)** Economics
7. **(C)** Sausan
8. **(B)** Witness for the defense
9. **(A)** She had cancer
10. **(D)** An Arab robe
11. **(C)** Ann Hammond
12. **(A)** Abu Nuwas
13. **(A)** Moozie
14. **(A)** Wad Rayyes
15. **(D)** He wants a cigarette
16. **(A)** Oxford
17. **(A)** A photo of Hosna and her sons
18. **(A)** Sheila Greenwood
19. **(B)** A wine glass
20. **(A)** Mahjoub
21. **(B)** A tribal woman murders her husband
22. **(D)** His fellow government employees are corrupt
23. **(A)** Because doing so won't solve his problems
24. **(D)** Twenty-four
25. **(C)** He finishes the last lines

ClassicNotes

Getting you the grade since 1999™

ClassicNotes

GradeSaver™

Getting you the grade since 1999™

Other ClassicNotes from GradeSaver™

Oliver Twist
On Liberty
On the Road
One Day in the Life of Ivan Denisovich
One Flew Over the Cuckoo's Nest
One Hundred Years of Solitude
Oroonoko
Othello
Our Town
The Outsiders
Pale Fire
Pamela: Or Virtue Rewarded
Paradise Lost
A Passage to India
The Pearl
Percy Shelley: Poems
Perfume: The Story of a Murderer
Persepolis: The Story of a Childhood
Persuasion
Phaedra
Phaedrus
The Piano Lesson
The Picture of Dorian Gray
Poe's Poetry
Poe's Short Stories
Poems of W.B. Yeats: The Rose
Poems of W.B. Yeats: The Tower
The Poems of William Blake
The Poetry of Robert Frost
The Poisonwood Bible
Pope's Poems and Prose
Portrait of the Artist as a Young Man
Pride and Prejudice
The Prince
The Professor's House
Prometheus Bound
Pudd'nhead Wilson
Pygmalion
Rabbit, Run
A Raisin in the Sun
The Real Life of Sebastian Knight
Rebecca
The Red Badge of Courage
The Remains of the Day
The Republic
Rhinoceros
Richard II
Richard III
The Rime of the Ancient Mariner
Rip Van Winkle and Other Stories
The Road
Robinson Crusoe
Roll of Thunder, Hear My Cry
Romeo and Juliet
A Room of One's Own
A Room With a View
A Rose For Emily and Other Short Stories
Rosencrantz and Guildenstern Are Dead
Salome
The Scarlet Letter
The Scarlet Pimpernel
The Seagull
Season of Migration to the North
The Secret Life of Bees
Secret Sharer
Sense and Sensibility
A Separate Peace
Shakespeare's Sonnets
Shantaram
Short Stories of Ernest Hemingway
Siddhartha
Silas Marner
Sir Gawain and the Green Knight
Sister Carrie
Six Characters in Search of an Author
Slaughterhouse Five
Snow Falling on Cedars
The Social Contract
Something Wicked This Way Comes
Song of Roland
Song of Solomon
Songs of Innocence and of Experience

For our full list of over 250 Study Guides, Quizzes, Sample College Application Essays, Literature Essays and E-texts, visit:

www.gradesaver.com

Printed in Great Britain
by Amazon

59800542R00059